Hello, America

A Refugee's Journey from Auschwitz to the New World

By Livia Bitton-Jackson

Simon Pulse
New York   London   Toronto   Sydney

SIMON PULSE

An imprint of Simon & Schuster Children's Publishing Division

1230 Avenue of the Americas, New York, NY 10020

Copyright © 2005 by Livia Bitton-Jackson

All rights reserved, including the right of reproduction in whole or in part in any form.

SIMON PULSE and colophon are registered trademarks of Simon & Schuster, Inc.

Also available in a Simon & Schuster Books for Young Readers hardcover edition.

Designed by Greg Stadnyk

The text of this book was set in Bembo.

Manufactured in the United States of America

First Simon Pulse edition July 2006

2 4 6 8 10 9 7 5 3

The Library of Congress has cataloged the hardcover edition as follows:

Jackson, Livia Bitton.

Hello, America / Livia Bitton-Jackson.

p. cm.

ISBN: 978-0-689-86755-2 (hc.)

1. Jackson, Livia Bitton. 2. Jews—New York (State)—New York—Biography.
3. Holocaust survivors—New York (State)—New York—Biography. 4. Refugees,
German—New York (State)—New York—Biography. 5. Immigrants—New York
(State)—New York—Biography. I. Title.

F128.9.J5J33 2004

940.53'18'092—dc22   2004014495

ISBN: 978-1-4169-1625-3 (pbk.)

Dedicated to the United States of America
and to the young women and men who do
their share to defend this most mighty
bulwark of freedom and decency.

———————————

I have received literally hundreds of inquiries from young readers about my life in America. Their intelligent questions, eager curiosity and touching concern served inspiration for this third sequel of my life story. I wish to express my heartfelt gratitude for the wonderful gift their letters have given me.

Simultaneously, I wish to thank VP Brenda Bowen at Simon & Schuster, my editor Alyssa Eisner, and my former editor Jessica Schulte for their brilliant, enthusiastic guidance and encouragement.

Chapter One

NEW YORK HARBOR, 1951

The day breaks as the SS *General Stuart* rapidly slices through the mist toward New York Harbor. With baited breath I watch the coastline approach. A moist wind slaps my hair against my cheeks, and my fingers feel numb from the intensity of my grip on the rail, testing reality. Is this a dream, or am I really standing on the upper deck of the ship drawing nearer and nearer to America? Today is Sabbath, just like when we set sail eight days ago. We started our journey on the holy day of Sabbath and we are completing it on Sabbath. God, is this a divine message . . . an omen?

The waters near the shore are calm, and I feel wonderful. The seasickness is gone. The turbulent ocean with its infinite majesty is behind us, spanning the abyss between our past and our future. Between homelessness in Europe and the promise of a home in America.

America, will you be my home? Will you embrace me as a daughter yearning to belong, an equal among equals, or will I forever remain a stranger, as on the other side of the ocean? Will you grant me my fervent desire of going to school once again? Will you grant me my secret ambition to become a teacher?

Am I dreaming too wild a dream?

Elli, my little sister . . . always impetuous . . . always dreaming . . . with your head always in the clouds. It's my brother's voice; I can hear it as if he were standing next to me. My brother Bubi! Oh, I can't wait to see him! How soon will I see him?

The pier is not too far now, and I can see a statuesque image gradually precipitate out of the fog. The Statue of Liberty! There is no mistake about it: As the boat moves along the pier, she emerges out of the haze in her full glory. How beautiful she is! I can see her clearly now. I can see her right hand holding the famous torch . . . the torch of liberty.

"Look, Mommy. There. There, on the horizon. Can you see it? The Statue of Liberty! Oh, Mommy! Did you think we'd live to see this sight?"

"Yes," Mother says softly, and there is a catch in her voice. "I can see it. . . . It's so hard to believe. And yet it is true. Thank God for having reached this moment."

I put my arms about her. "Oh, Mommy. I can't believe we've made it!"

Others have seen the statue too, and a cheer rises among the ranks of refugees storming the rails. Several men whip off their caps and someone begins to sing, and the cheer turns into many different songs, many different anthems—a basket of melodies rising into the mist.

"The American anthem," I shout. "Who can sing the American anthem?"

But no one hears me. No one knows the new anthem of our new homeland: The refugees keep singing the anthems of their hearts in different languages, a cacophony of tongues. The deck is full now . . . men, women, and little children . . . singing, faces red from the wind and wet with tears. It is one song—the song of the refugees coming home.

"Oh, Mommy. I can't believe we've made it!"

"Not yet. We haven't made it yet." Gently she frees herself from my embrace. "Elli, let's go and gather our things," she says cheerfully. "Let's hurry. We shouldn't be among the last to step ashore."

I nod. "Let's hurry and be among the first!"

We go below to pack our things, and as we maneuver our luggage toward the upper deck, Mother is caught up in a human tide sweeping her toward the gangway.

"Mom, wait! I can't go yet. I can't leave without saying good-bye to Captain McGregor and Steward McDonald." Pushing against the current, Mother and I manage to reach the staterooms. But the officers are nowhere to be seen. As we drag our luggage toward the mess deck, I hear a familiar voice in the crowd.

"There you are! Look at you! All recovered." The captain's eyes sparkle with playful good humor. "All peachy pink and ready to go!"

"Yes, I'm fine now. The seasickness was gone as soon as we slowed down for landing."

"I know, I know. It's the nature of the beast. Where are you heading?"

"We have family in Brooklyn."

"Brooklyn? Do you have a passport? You have to cross a bridge to get to Brooklyn, and for that you need a special passport. Brooklyn is foreign territory."

"Oh, no! We have no passports at all. Our status is 'stateless.' None of the refugees have passports!" Tension tightens my stomach.

The captain's eyes now have a dark, wicked glow. "Then you cannot get to Brooklyn. You'll have to stay right here!"

Seeing my panic, he locks me in a bear hug. "Oh, I was only kidding. May God be with you wherever you go, Miss Friedman. Thanks for your help. You did a hell of a job. I'll miss you on my next crossing."

What does *kidding* mean? I hope it means he was not serious about Brooklyn being a foreign land.

As Captain McGregor holds me in his arms, I remember our first meeting.

Was it only a week ago Thursday that the exciting news rippled through the ranks of the refugees in the Bremerhaven transit camp that our boat had arrived and we would be boarding on Saturday morning? But Saturday is Sabbath, when it is forbidden by Jewish law to board a ship! Mommy and I were faced with the agonizing problem until early Friday morning when I proposed a solution: I would volunteer to work as an interpreter on the ship and request permission for the two of us to board on Friday instead of Saturday. Although delighted with the idea, Mommy was dubious. But the captain miraculously accepted my offer and bade us to board immediately together with the crew.

And now here we are, ready to step ashore in America, the land of freedom. Far behind us is the blood-soaked soil of Europe, the graveyard of all I had loved—my family, my friends, my childhood.

It has been a long journey. When did it begin? Did it begin when young American soldiers liberated me, a fourteen-year-old skeleton, from the German prison train, offering us, walking corpses, the gift of life . . . of hope?

Or did it begin before the war, when Papa clutched in his hands the Czechoslovak passport that promised to transform his dreams of America into reality? But as the shadows of war loomed ever larger, America was beckoning from an ever-receding horizon, until Hitler's march into Prague sent the U.S. Embassy packing, delivering a final, fatal blow to our hopes. And so instead of America, my father's journey ended in a mass grave in Bergen-Belsen.

The three of us, my mother, my brother, and I, dazed survivors of the empire of death, continued the journey. My brother left for America four years ago on a student visa, while Mother and I wandered through Europe, moving from one refugee camp to another in the American Zone of Germany, getting ever closer to the American dream. Until that memorable Friday more than a week ago when in the port of Bremen a small ship bobbing on the waves came into view, the name SS *General Stuart* clearly visible on the bow.

Belowdecks, no sooner did Mom and I arrange our bedclothes under the pillows and tuck our luggage neatly under the bunk than a trimly uniformed marine officer appeared and bade me to follow him up the companion-way to the captain's office.

Captain McGregor greeted me jovially and pointed to a desk in the corner with an old gray Olympic typewriter among stacks of paper.

"Here, Miss Friedman, is your office, complete with typewriter," he said crisply. "First we have to compose special lists according to nationalities. Here is the passenger list. Nationality is listed next to each name. Please sort the names by nationality groups and type up a separate list for each. We also need a list of children below the age of fifteen—for the children's dining room. You'll find ages listed next to names. Your skills as interpreter will be needed to sort out those who require a meatless diet. Those passengers will eat in the meatless dining room. We'll compile that list after the passengers board early tomorrow morning. That list can be typed up then and immediately posted with the kitchen crew."

"I can sort out those who require a meatless diet," I remarked carefully. "But I can't type up the list tomorrow morning. It's part of what I mentioned this morning about Sabbath observance. I'm not allowed to type on the Sabbath."

"I understand. No problem. One of the stewards will do the typing. Can you get the information from the passengers and dictate it? Is that okay?"

I nodded and settled down at the ancient typewriter. Conscious of the limited time at my disposal, I plunged into work. At noon the captain stopped at my desk.

"Young lady, I'm sorry to interrupt your work, but it's lunchtime. I'm here to invite you and your mother to join me and the rest of the crew at my table for lunch."

"Oh. Thank you, Captain," I replied awkwardly. "I wish we could join you. But my mother and I, we eat kosher food only."

"Whadd'ya know!" he exclaimed. "Our first couple of meatless customers! No problem. I'll tell the cook. He'll take care of you."

The jolly company, cold salad, cottage cheese, and canned corn made for a delightful lunch. And something else: dessert. A frozen, dark brown brick painstakingly sliced into squares by the cook. "What is it?" The crew was greatly amused to discover that I had never seen or tasted chocolate ice cream. One by one they generously piled their portions of the frozen delicacy on my plate. Only later did I find out that they all hated this chocolate ice cream, and were delighted to find easy prey!

As the afternoon wore on, a gentle tap on my shoulder startled me. It was Mother.

"Elli, it's sunset. Time for Sabbath. You must stop typing."

"Okay, Mom," I reassured her. "I will join you below deck as soon as I've delivered the lists to the captain."

When I arrived belowdecks I found that Mother had fashioned a small table out of a footstool and arranged the two candles she brought along, using bottle caps for candleholders. Her face took on a special glow as she lit the candles, and then, covering her eyes with her hands, she recited the Hebrew blessing over the flickering lights.

Our dark little corner below deck was transformed into a circle of radiance.

The sound of hurried footsteps broke the spell. Taken aback at the sight of the candles, the first steward mumbled an embarrassed apology. "Sorry, Miss, but you're needed above to meet the kitchen crew and explain to them about kosher."

Captain McGregor introduced me to a large group of marines I recognized from lunch. To my surprise they listened avidly to my talk on the rules of kashruth and asked penetrating questions, and the hour was quite late by the time First Steward McDonald broke up the discussion. As the marines dispersed with cheers and catcalls, Captain McGregor chuckled. "Hey, young lady, you were quite a hit!"

It was past midnight when I finally joined Mother in the bunk and dropped into bed exhausted yet exhilarated from my remarkable experience in the ship's kitchen. Mother listened quietly to my story about the marines' reaction to my talk, then remarked wryly, "I would have never imagined that a lecture on kosher food would make such an exhilarating topic."

At dawn Steward McDonald appeared at my bunk. "Miss Friedman, our customers are boarding. We need an interpreter to issue directives."

"I'll be with you in a minute," I mumbled hoarsely and climbed off my bed. Thank God I was too tired the night before to get undressed. In less than a minute I was ready to follow the first steward.

"As you know, we are accommodating them by ethnic

groups. Hopefully this will make for a more successful passage." He whispered as we climbed the metal stairs, confiding, "Our last passage with refugees was dismal."

Masses of refugees ascended the gangplank. From the lists I'd put together I knew that they spoke Slovenian, Czech, Ukrainian, Yiddish, German, Hungarian, Polish, Romanian, and Italian. Hungarian, German, and Yiddish were easy. And my knowledge of Slovak helped me to communicate also in Slovenian, Czech, Ukrainian, and Polish—all Slavic languages. But I could speak neither Romanian nor Italian. What was I going to do?

"Do you have a pad and a red pencil?" I asked Steward McDonald.

Steward McDonald produced a red pencil and took my dictation in large block letters: CHI PARLA ITALIANO? "What does it mean?"

"I hope it means 'Who speaks Italian?' Italian would help us also with Romanian."

I raised the pad above the crowd, and almost instantly a voice called out, *"Io parlo Italiano."*

The voice belonged to a young Serb from Zagreb, who besides Italian and his native tongue also knew German, spanning a linguistic proficiency in the three main language families—Germanic, Slavic, and Romance—a perfect combination for communicating with the refugees.

The young man from Zagreb, his name was Stanko Vranich, seemed to have phenomenal organizational ability, and with his help the boarding proceeded smoothly. Stanko's support boosted my sense of competence, and the two of us had all the refugees settled in their respective quarters in less than three hours.

"I should hire you on a permanent basis," the captain chuckled. "We could do with such orderly boarding on every passage."

"Meet my senior partner." I introduced the slim young man whose narrow auburn mustache partially concealed a harelip. "This is Mr. Vranich. I couldn't have done it without him." As the officers saluted him, Stanko courteously bowed his head.

The rest of the morning kept me busy dashing up and down between the hold, the staterooms, the kitchen, and the mess deck, conveying requests for extra blankets, cots, buckets, food items. It was almost noon as I was climbing up the companionway to the upper deck right behind Captain McGregor, when suddenly an incomprehensible surge of nausea sent the contents of my stomach up my throat. Luckily there was a bucket of sand nearby and I managed to direct the charge into it, and continued up the stairs without the captain noticing. Wow! It must have been the canned fish I had for dinner. Or that mountain of chocolate ice cream! Thank goodness the captain didn't seem to notice!

But once we were up deck Captain McGregor burst into uproarious laughter.

"God almighty, you've got it bad! Poor devil, right at the start."

"What do you mean? What have I got?"

"A bad case of what's called seasickness"

"Seasickness? What are you talking about?"

"You're green to the gills. That's what I'm talking about!"

The next moment another excruciating wave of nausea hurled my stomach to the roof of my mouth, and what was left of its contents shot out like a salvo of bullets. In panic and shame I doubled over another bucket of sand at the side of the rail. God, I wanted to die that instant.

"I apologize. This has never . . . never happened to me before," I managed to sputter.

"You've never been seasick before." The captain's chuckle was no longer mocking. He placed a comforting hand on my shoulder and whispered an astounding confession: "I've been at sea for fifteen years, and I get seasick on every passage. Just haven't started yet. Too early."

"How can one be seasick before sailing? While the ship is at anchor in the harbor?"

Now the captain was rocking with laughter. "At anchor? We've been sailing for over an hour!"

It could not be. I'd asked Mommy to come and tell me when we were sailing. She'd promised to warn me in time.

I slid my hand into my pocket to touch my little parcel, my last gift to Germany. It was there. A piece of paper wrapped about a small rock and tied with a yellow ribbon the color of the *Judenstern,* the canary yellow Jewish star I was forced to wear . . . in readiness. My private message to Germany—to its gas chambers, its mass graves, its fields of grass above mutilated corpses, its forests concealing the shrieks of the tormented. For the

11

moment of departure . . . my gesture of farewell.

I ran to the railing. The rock wrapped in my special message was waiting in my pocket, ready for my sacred ritual. The coastline was barely visible in the distance. Rough waves churned at the stern of the ship as it rapidly moved away from Germany. I raised my hand high, ready to fling its contents. It was of no use. The coastline was beyond range. I dropped the missive into my pocket.

For years I had planned this gesture of last farewell in the name of all who are buried in this accursed soil and who, unlike me, were unable to leave it. Why was I deprived of my good-bye to Germany?

I ran belowdecks. "Mommy, why didn't you warn me in time?" I cried with bitter disappointment. "You promised you would call me the minute the ship sailed!"

"I'm sorry, my daughter," Mother said apologetically. "I was taking a rest. You know *Shabbat* afternoon I always doze off. And when I awoke, it was too late. There was no point in disturbing you. You were so busy. . . ."

I remembered another lost farewell, another bitter confrontation with Mommy, and I felt my heart break all over again. *It's early spring. . . . I am standing in my nightgown, barefoot in the chill of the dark dawn . . . hear the beating of the horses' hooves, the carriages clattering in the distance. The last carriage is dimly visible, and through a haze of rising dust I can see Papa's silhouette among several other men in the departing carriage. . . . Powerless in the face of my savage grief, I shriek, "Mommy, how could you do this to me? How could you rob me of my good-bye? Why didn't you wake me as you promised?"*

12

Years had passed since then, but the shriek of pain remained trapped in my soul.

The ship was heading for the open sea, and the coastline had disappeared. Captain McGregor was no longer on deck. I went below to look for him either in the stateroom or in his office. Perhaps he had some chore for me. I had to keep busy. I had been told that's the best antidote for seasickness. It's also the best antidote for heartache.

Now the captain shakes hands with Mother. "God bless you too, ma'am. You've got a great lass here." Then he turns to me with a wink. "Translate it for me, will you?"

Two young marines offer to help with our luggage, and we follow them down the gangway.

Unexpectedly we find ourselves surrounded by the carnival atmosphere of a cavernous enclosure. Colorful flags and banners with bold lettering—NYANA, HIAS, NIMBUS, AMERICO-ITALIA—are brandished by representatives of sponsor groups; whistles and catcalls, sobs and cheerful shrieks of recognition fill the air. More and more arrivals surge forward, scrambling with zealous obedience toward the banners matching the tags in their buttonholes. Loud emotional farewells, frantic waving of hands, tearful promises of contact—the last throes of friendships and romances forged during the ocean crossing.

In a daze I push ahead, making way for Mother toward a group gathered about the banner of our sponsor, HIAS.

"What's the meaning of HIAS?" a voice calls from

behind, and I respond before turning my head and checking who has asked the question.

"It's an acronym for Hebrew Immigrant Aid Society."

All at once I recognize my Yugoslav hero, Stanko Vranich. He is sporting a large tag with the letters NYANA.

"Ah, it's you! You are with NYANA? And what does NYANA stand for?"

"New York Association for New Americans. Can you see the sign in the far corner on the right? I'm on my way there." I crane my neck, but in the sea of people I cannot find it. "I just came by to say good-bye, Miss Friedman. I wanted to wish you good luck."

The firmness of Stanko's handshake comes as a surprise. It is out of character for the soft-spoken translator.

"Thank you, Mr. Vranich." I smile in return. "I hope you will achieve your goals." During the last two days of our journey, Stanko and I discovered that we shared many ambitions, dreams. "I hope all your dreams will materialize."

"And yours!" A cloud sails across Stanko's smiling face and, with regret in his tone, he declares, "Had I applied for HIAS sponsorship in time, we would now be going off together. But I found out about HIAS too late, after I had been accepted by NYANA."

HIAS? Stanko is Jewish? Why didn't he say anything? Stanko now drops his luggage and extends both hands, holding my right hand in a solid grip. "But I didn't know you then, Miss Friedman. I hope you will find happiness in America."

"Much luck to you, too," I say with sincerity. Stanko bows his head and, gripping his luggage, darts in the direction of the NYANA banner. A second later he turns back and shouts above the din. "I'll contact HIAS to inquire about you. You don't mind?" I shake my head. No, I don't mind. As a matter of fact, I hope he'll do that. I hope I'll see Stanko again.

Mother and I crowd about the counter of an enthusiastic HIAS representative registering names and vital statistics, and a stream of shipboard acquaintances pass by for last-minute handshakes, last-minute good wishes.

All at once, in the colorful kaleidoscope of faces I spot a smile and my heart gives a jolt. Now the face disappears in the crowd, but the smile lingers before my eyes. . . . I could not have imagined that smile. It was there a moment ago.

"Mommy, I saw Bubi! I'm sure he's here somewhere in the crowd."

"Bubi? What are you talking about? Elli, stop fantasizing. You know it's impossible for your brother to be here. Today is Sabbath. How could he get here? In New York distances are great. It's not possible to make the trip to the pier on foot. I told you not to expect him, not to drive yourself crazy. Please relax; be patient. You'll see him tonight after the Sabbath will be over. Or tomorrow."

The glimpse of my brother's face in the crowd has obliterated everything else. Suddenly everything is a blur, the crowd, the HIAS representative, the stream of leave-takers. Only my brother's smile remains in sharp focus. It was there. I know it. I must reach it.

Despite Mother's indignant dismissal of what I have seen, I begin pushing and shoving and making my way through the crowd . . . in the direction of the smile. I can see him clearly now! Tall, handsome . . . different. Like an American, in a gray overcoat and a wide-brimmed hat.

"Bubi! Bubi!"

In our embrace four years of separation dissolve into thin air. Four years of waiting, struggle, anguish, are over. Thank you, my dear God.

"Elli! Is it really you? I can barely recognize you. You've grown . . . changed. . . . Where's Mommy?"

"There. The lady in the dark blue overcoat. Can you see her now? Come, let me take you to her. She won't believe her eyes."

I clutch Bubi's hand and drag him through the crowd to the spot where Mother is standing with her back to us. When Bubi stands before her, Mother's eyes and mouth open wide in astonishment.

"Here he is, Mommy . . ."

"Bubi?!"

Mother clutches us both to her body, her arms encircling us, holding us tighter and tighter, and the three of us begin to sway in a dance of rebirth. Like a cluster of grapes dangling from a vine branch on a patch of brand-new soil.

Chapter Two

MY FIRST DAY IN AMERICA

"Oh, Papa . . . Papa!" I shriek, and throw my arms about the shy stranger whose face now materializes in the crowd. He has high cheekbones . . . a square jaw . . . hazel eyes. He is tall and lean, and his shoulders are wide. "Papa!" I cannot control my sobs. How I miss those high cheekbones . . . that square jaw . . . those hazel eyes. How I miss those wide, athletic shoulders. Oh, Papa . . . I still cannot believe that you will not emerge from the hazy dawn into which you disappeared without a good-bye. I can't believe that you're gone forever. For me your return will forever remain a possible dream.

My outburst stuns everyone present, especially the tall, lean man with hazel eyes, Papa's brother, who awkwardly tolerates my embrace, and then with an embarrassed cough moves behind the stately woman next to him. This must be Aunt Lilly, my uncle's wife. She looks different from in the photographs included in those curious blue envelopes that came from America. A woman of great vivacity, now her smile fades and her eyes brim with tears.

My shocking display injects into our first meeting the very thing we were determined to avoid, at least for now . . . to leave unmentioned the unmentionable. Aunt Lilly takes the first step at damage control. She wipes her tears and extends both arms in an expansive welcome.

"Laura! Elli! Welcome to America."

For Mother this is a reunion with my uncle and aunt after an absence of more than twenty years, years before Uncle Abish left Europe for America with his wife and young son. The two women—Mother, tall, slim, and slightly stooped, and Aunt Lilly, rather short and slightly plump—hold each other at arm's length, assess each other, measure the telltale signs of the years that passed, then fall into each other's arms.

"Thank God you've arrived. We've been waiting and waiting," Aunt Lilly shouts above the din.

"How did you get here on the Sabbath?" Mother asks in surprise.

"On foot. Our apartment is within walking distance. I hope you're not too tired to make the walk. I believe it's worth the effort, Laurie, Ellike. A good Sabbath meal awaits you at our house," Aunt Lilly's eyes twinkle happily.

A Sabbath meal! The words reach me through a haze of fatigue, excitement, years of distance. An invitation to a Sabbath meal—how long has it been? How long has it been since we experienced anything as festive, as heart-warmingly mundane? As welcoming?

"What about our luggage?" Mother asks.

"Perhaps the HIAS people will let you store your things at their place here until the end of the Sabbath.

Your cousin Tommy can drive here after the Sabbath is over and collect them."

The HIAS representatives kindly consent to store our luggage, and Mother and I follow our hosts out of the dank air of the reception hall into brilliant sunshine.

A stroll through the streets of New York! I feel as if I were walking on a cloud. The plainness of the Lower East Side does not mar the radiance of the moment: The walk from the pier to my aunt and uncle's flat on Avenue D remains one of the most exciting, one of the most memorable, occasions of my life.

But I'm curious. Where is grand, lavishly rich America I've heard so much about? Where are the wide boulevards, the big flashy cars, the skyscrapers, the Americans dressed in brash colors and styles I have seen in the movies?

"This section of the city is not representative of America. Or New York, for that matter," Bubi explains. "Don't worry, *Leanyka*. You'll see skyscrapers and wide boulevards and flashily dressed people," he promises. "In time you'll see *everything*, experience *everything*," he adds in the somewhat patronizing, somewhat mocking tone I remember so well. It's a thrill to be called *Leanyka*, little girl, once again. After so many years.

"This is a very big city, a metropolis. It takes time and patience. Are you still impatient, still a bit impetuous?"

Mommy walks ahead with Aunt Lilly and Uncle Abish. My inexcusable explosion at the pier opened a breach in the dam and the questions, the burning, apprehensive questions, begin to filter through. Bubi and I walk behind them and overhear the dreaded, inevitable exchange. The three of them walk with their backs hunched, Mommy bracing herself for the questions, and they, the American relatives, bracing themselves for the answers.

Uncle Abish and Aunt Lilly have been totally cut off from their families in Europe since the outbreak of the war in 1939. And when the war was over and contacts were reestablished worldwide, they discovered that for them there was no family to contact. All members of Aunt Lilly's family perished. For Uncle Abish, whose mother, brother, sister, brother-in-law, and their five children were put to death, we—the dead brother's widow and two children—are his only family now. For them we are the live witnesses, cinders saved from the fire, to tell the story.

As we walk Bubi resumes his role as big brother, teacher, my ultimate font of all knowledge. First comes a lesson in local geography. He explains that New York City is divided into five boroughs, and teaches me their names—Manhattan, Brooklyn, Bronx, Queens, and Richmond, or Staten Island.

"We are now in the borough of Manhattan. Aunt Celia and Uncle Martin live in the borough of Brooklyn."

Aunt Celia is Mom's sister. We plan to stay with her and her husband after our visit with Uncle Abish and Aunt Lilly.

"I know. Now that Aunt Celia and Uncle Martin have invited us to live with them until we find our own apartment . . . we have to get to Brooklyn. . . . But is it true that we need a passport to travel from Manhattan to Brooklyn?" I ask. "Mommy and I have no passports. Officially our status is 'stateless.'"

"Who told you that you need a passport to go to Brooklyn?" Bubi asks in surprise.

"The ship's captain. He said Brooklyn was like a foreign country. You had to cross a bridge to get to Brooklyn. You needed a passport in order to cross that bridge."

"Really, he said that?" Bubi chuckles. "Little sister, he was pulling your leg—that's an American expression. He was joking. Brooklyn is part of New York City, just like Manhattan. It's true you have to cross a bridge because Manhattan is an island. No matter where you go from Manhattan, you have to cross a bridge. Even to the Bronx. Or Queens."

"The captain did say he was only 'kidding,'" I confide to my brother. "But I wasn't sure what *kidding* meant."

We finally arrive at my aunt and uncle's apartment. It is small but airy and spotlessly clean. The dining room table is covered with a heavy damask tablecloth and set with fine bone china dishes, heavy silver cutlery, and crystal drinking glasses. And the air is permeated with the aromas of a traditional Sabbath meal.

Cousin Tommy, my uncle and aunt's only son, arrives with family friends. The Goldsteins are compatriots from Hungary, and they give us a hearty welcome. Their two adolescent daughters, a thirteen- and a fifteen-year-old, are wearing lipstick and high-heel shoes!

Although they look their age, they are dressed like grown women.

We all settle down to the Sabbath feast. Aunt Lilly produces a stunning array of food—gefilte fish, chicken soup, roast beef, kugel, cholent, and schnitzel—all served on proper china platters and in bowls. There are drinks—wine, seltzer, and beer—in cut glasses. And the dessert—apple strudel and tea—is served on side plates and in dainty porcelain teacups!

My God. In America, time has stood still. Staggering amounts of food, consumed with apparent unconcern. Such a glut of food and drink . . . taken for granted! Here the war has never happened. Starvation, shortages . . . never happened. Here the unfathomable chasm between Before and After does not exist. Fine china, silverware, delicate teacups, damask tablecloth. So the Old World, the world of Before that for us had vanished without a trace, that for us had slid into the realm of never-never land, is actually the here and now in America. . . . It's alive and well in the New World!

Where do I belong? Will I ever span the chasm that separates these two realities? Will I ever learn to accept American luxuries without the inhibitions imposed by my memories of deprivation? Will I ever learn to live with this abundance as casually as the Americans do? Could I ever be like them?

"Mom, the strap on my left shoe broke," the older Goldstein girl announces.

"What a shame," the mother replies. "It's a new pair. I got them to go with the dress you're wearing."

"What am I to do? I can't walk in them with the strap broken!" she cries indignantly.

"I'll get you another pair on Monday. First thing," the mother promises, and the girl seems somewhat appeased.

"Can't you have the strap repaired?" I ask.

"In America we don't repair things," Mrs. Goldstein explains. "If something breaks, you buy a new one."

"Are there no shoe-repair shops here?"

"Repair shops are rare, and repair work is expensive. It's sometimes cheaper to buy a new pair of shoes. Or anything else, for that matter."

"And what happens to the broken item?"

"You throw it out."

"Throw it out?" I cry, taken aback. You throw out a pair of shoes just because the strap broke? I glance under the table to look at the shoes. They are a beautiful pair of cream-colored patent leather pumps. If only I could have such elegant shoes! I would repair the pump myself. It takes only a few stitches to sew on a strap. What a shame!

I am in shock. Wow! This is America ? Adolescent girls wearing lipstick and high heels! A beautiful pair of cream-colored patent leather pumps thrown out because the strap broke!

How does it feel to have a different pair of shoes for every outfit? How many pairs of shoes do these girls have? I have been happy with the one pair of shoes I own . . . forever grateful that they fit well . . . forever remembering the shoes I was forced to wear in the death camps, the agony of walking miles and miles in shoes two sizes too small. . . .

Will I ever forget the agony? Will I ever forget to thank God for granting me the luxury of a comfortable pair of shoes? Will I ever be like an American teenager and throw out a perfectly good pair of shoes because of a slight flaw?

God, help me make my way in America.

Chapter Three

BROADWAY

After the Goldstein family leaves with Tommy as their gallant escort, Aunt Lilly suggests that we all take a well-deserved rest till the evening, when Tommy would drive us to Brooklyn.

"I would rather go for a walk, if Bubi is willing to take me," I say and cast an imploring look in my brother's direction.

"Okay," Bubi agrees, and the two of us bid *Good Shabbes* to Mommy, Aunt Lilly, and Uncle Abish. "Where do you want to go?"

"Just walk . . . anywhere. Is there a park in the vicinity?"

"Not really."

For several minutes my brother and I walk in silence. There is so much to say after four years of separation, so many questions to ask. Where do I begin?

"I want to ask you . . ." My brother is the first to speak. "When you met Uncle Abish this morning at the pier, why did you cry on his shoulder, calling him Papa? Did you for a moment think he was Papa? Did he remind you of Papa so much? But he's not like our father at all, not in looks and not in personality. There's no resemblance."

All at once tears spring into my eyes. "To me there is. Everything about him reminds me of Papa, his body build, his high cheekbones, hazel eyes . . . there's an aura about him that's like Papa. Oh, Bubi, I miss him so much!"

"Ever since that scene at the pier, I've been thinking. You didn't get to know Papa very well . . . couldn't, really. You were very young when he was taken away. I had a chance to know him before it all started, but you . . . how much time did you spend with him? To get to know him?"

"But I did. He taught me to swim and to ride the bike. While you were away at school, he taught me to play chess. We would play for hours, late into the night. Do you remember the sports equipment—the rings, the chin-up bar, the swing—he fixed up in the yard and taught us to work out on them? I believe that's where my love of sport stems from."

How happy Papa was when I took to it like a duck to water . . . how proud. I was his kind of girl, he said. Ever since then wherever I have swum or ridden a bike, Papa has been beside me, cheering me on. I can hear his voice: *Go on, you're doing fine. . . . Just a little more! Don't give up. . . . Never give up!*

"Do you remember his dictionary of foreign words? We used to pore over it together, he, pointing out the origins of foreign words in Hungarian, and I, memorizing them. I believe that's where my love of foreign languages stems from."

The true source of my sense of kinship with Papa I can't reveal to my brother. During those years that he was away at school I overheard Mother say to Papa how Bubi was just like her family, her brothers, whereas I was just like Papa. "Bubi has a good head," I heard him concede. "But Elli has *Sitzfleisch*. She has perseverance. Sometimes, in the long run, perseverance gets you farther than a good head."

"Yes, I remember the dictionary of foreign words," Bubi says with a smile. "He was fascinated with the etymology of words. And of course I remember the sports equipment in the yard, how much he loved to exercise. You liked that kind of stuff. . . . I must confess I didn't."

We walk on the colorless streets of the Lower East Side and talk of the Danube River back in Czechoslovakia, of its silvery blue ripples, of the brilliant green of the forest, and of the long, lazy summer afternoons when after a vigorous swim Papa would play soccer with us in the grass, then draw my brother into the shade of the woods flanking the river and study with him the portion of the week from the Pentateuch or a page of the Talmud.

"I'll never forget the passage of the Talmud that we studied together on that last night, before he was taken away," Bubi reminisces, and his voice is somewhat hoarse with emotion. "He said, 'This is how I wish to part from you, learning a passage of the Talmud. Remember this passage when you remember me. . . .'"

Bubi falls silent as we stroll on the faded brick sidewalk past shuttered storefronts. All at once the elongated shadows of the tenement houses plunge the street into twilight, and Bubi is taken aback with the realization of the late hour.

"We must turn back," he says now with urgency. "We've wandered too far. We must get back to Uncle Abish's house before the end of the Sabbath."

We have wandered too far indeed. Although Bubi and I now gallop like racehorses through darkened streets and alleyways, it takes us more than half an hour to reach our relatives' flat.

"Where have you been?" The entire Friedman family is racked with worry.

"You can stop worrying," Bubi the cool pragmatist reassures the excitable Hungarian bunch. "We are here, safe and sound, and *Shabbes* is not even over yet."

In fact, *Shabbes* has been over for some time, and Tommy has gone to bring his car and drive us to the pier for our luggage en route to Brooklyn.

Mommy and I bid a fond farewell to our American family, and they promise to come visit us in Brooklyn.

My heart is brimming with excitement as I am sitting in the front seat of Tommy's new car, in between Mommy and the driver. These amazing American cars are so wide there is room for three people in the seat. What an exhilarating experience, driving in the face of oncoming traffic, a sea of blinding light beams and a cacophony of honking horns.

"Is New York City like this every night?" I ask.

"Saturday night is. On Saturday night people go out. People from the boroughs drive to Manhattan to theaters, movie houses, concerts, restaurants. We're lucky to be heading in the opposite direction so we're not stuck in a traffic jam. Soon we'll reach the Brooklyn Bridge. You'll see all the traffic on the bridge. It's tremendous at this hour."

"I have never seen so many cars in my life!" Mother cries.

Tommy's car rolls onto the ramp off the bridge and soon makes its way to a beautiful boulevard, a wide, tree-lined street stretching on and on for miles.

"Is this Broadway?"

"Broadway? Oh, no! We're in Brooklyn now. We crossed the Brooklyn Bridge twenty minutes ago. Broadway is in Manhattan."

"What street is this?"

"This is Ocean Avenue. It's the street where Aunt Celia and Uncle Martin live," my brother calls from the backseat.

"Really? I didn't expect such wide streets in Brooklyn. I thought . . ."

"That's the meaning of *avenue*," my brother explains, "a wide street, like a boulevard."

"Is Broadway much wider than this? Is it far from here?"

"Do you want to see Broadway?" Tommy asks. "I can take you tomorrow, if you want."

"Will you? I can't wait to see Broadway, and the cloud scrapers. Papa told me that on Broadway there are cloud scrapers, buildings over a hundred stories high."

"There's one building like that," Tommy says. "The Empire State Building. It's a hundred and ten stories high. But it's not exactly on Broadway."

"And the word is *skyscraper,*" Bubi pipes up again in the back.

I remember that New York was Papa's city of dreams, and he hoped one day to make it to New York. But I must not talk about it. Not now. I must not tell Tommy that Daddy promised to buy me the prettiest dress on Broadway. Papa would point to a picture of one of the staggering, tall buildings. "This is over a hundred stories high. Can you fathom a building so tall? One day you and I will walk up on Broadway and turn our heads to see the top of that building that touches the clouds. I guess that's why they call them cloud scrapers. Can you see the big shop windows?" He would go on. "We'll go into one of those big, fancy shops on Broadway and I'll buy you the prettiest dress." "Oh, Papa," I would exclaim, and give him a tight hug. "Oh, Papa. I love you so."

It was our game during the dark, difficult times. By then we had been waiting for more than two years for our turn on the American quota. The war was raging and Hitler's armies were drawing ever nearer, spreading panic in their wake. And there was no reply from the American Embassy to our inquiries as to when, for God's sake, we would get entry visas to America. It seemed hopeless, yet Father kept up our morale with tales of the dazzling metropolis we would reach "someday."

"Well, this is it." Tommy says as he pulls alongside the

curb and parks the car in front of a large, impressive building. "2010 Ocean Avenue."

"This is where Aunt Celia lives?"

"Yes," Bubi answers. "This is the house."

I gaze in amazement at the stately building and follow Mother up three or four wide stone steps to the entrance and into the spacious lobby. The two boys follow behind, carrying our luggage to the far end of the hall. I cannot believe my eyes. The courtly look of the hall with its polished floor and fireplace reminds me of opulent, turn-of-the-century buildings in Vienna. This is more like the America I have dreamed about.

We climb the stairs at the far end of the lobby to the first floor. Bubi rings the bell on a door in the left-hand corner of the hallway, and I feel my throat tighten. In seconds the door opens wide, and Aunt Celia, as tall and as beautiful as I remember her, rushes to meet us.

"Laura! Elli!"

"Celia!"

We cling to each other in exaltation tinged with pain. I remember another reunion, in another place, at another time. How long has it been? We are locked in a silent embrace, and all at once the dark hallway is transformed. I'm in the midst of *a desiccated vista battered by blinding, scorching sun . . . and in the distance I can see a tall, sticklike figure meander about, shouting, "Laura! Laura! Laura!" It's my aunt, Mom's younger sister, still stunning in the drab prison uniform with shaven head. "Aunt Celia!" She looks at me uncomprehending, locks me in a frantic embrace. "Elli! Little Elli, you are here? How can it be? And your mother . . . where's your mother?" Her tears smudge my face as I lead her to the dusty hollow where Mother has fallen asleep. Celia crawls into the hole next to her and the two sisters greet each other with silent panic, hold each other in a silent clasp, weeping silently in the scorching dust hole of Auschwitz, the most dreaded concentration camp . . . only to be separated again.*

How long has it been? And now here we are, after years of longing, the three of us once again locked in a tight embrace. . . . But now in a new world, at the threshold of a new life.

The ecstasy of our reunion is marred by the agony of remembering. Our tears of joy are mingled with tears of pain for the agonizing losses we suffered since that meeting in Auschwitz during the first day of our arrival. The ghost of seventeen-year-old Imre, Aunt Celia and Uncle Martin's cherished only son, is locked within our embrace as, still sobbing, Aunt Celia leads us into her American home.

The exuberance in Uncle Martin's eyes as he greets us and the two boys is in sharp contrast to the telltale signs of grief—the deep lines in the boyish face and the streaks of gray in the once unruly red hair.

"How is my favorite chess partner?" he asks as he hugs Mother. And when it is my turn to embrace my beloved uncle, I break into sobs almost as uncontrollable as when meeting Uncle Abish at the pier. What's the matter with me? Why can't I keep my emotions under control? In front of my new cousin . . . how embarrassing. And in front of my brother . . . he used to call me a crybaby, but now, thankfully, he does not say anything.

My weeping makes Uncle Martin's eyes turn red, and he whispers, "There's so much to talk about. . . . Thank God you're here."

In the sparse, well-lit kitchen the table is set for six. But my brother, Bubi, and my cousin Tommy decline Aunt and Uncle's invitation to dinner. Bubi has to return to his studies at Yeshiva University, and Tommy offers to give him a lift.

"Tomorrow at nine," Tommy promises. "I'll come pick you up and take you to see Broadway. And to the Empire State Building."

After dinner the four of us talk and talk late into the night. There is so much to say, so much to remember. And so much not to.

It is after midnight when Celia and Martin open the Castro convertible couch in their living room, and it becomes a double bed for Mother and me. When we finally bid each other good night and I crawl under the covers, I find it difficult to fall asleep. What a long day it has been! The deluge of new impressions surges like a torrent in my mind's eye. I stay awake thinking about all I've experienced since our arrival this morning.

And then there's something else that keeps me from sleep. Every half an hour or so there is a thunderous clatter like the rattle of an approaching and departing train. How can one sleep through all this noise?

"That's the elevated train," Aunt Celia explains in the morning. "The Brighton Line of the subway system, just about four blocks from here."

"You'll get used to the noise very fast," Uncle reassures

me, laughing. "In time you won't be able to sleep without it."

The four of us have breakfast together—orange juice, rye bread with cream cheese, and instant coffee with milk from a carton!—my first American breakfast. Then Uncle Martin leaves for his workshop where he manufactures children's hats.

Tommy is prompt. At nine o'clock sharp he appears on my aunt's doorstep, ready for the day's outing, just as he promised.

Broadway is not as wide open a boulevard as I thought it would be. And Tommy is right: There are no skyscrapers, only ordinary two-, three-, and four-story buildings.

"Why is it called Broadway? It's not very broad."

"I don't know. There must be some story attached to the name. There almost always is."

But when we reach mid-Manhattan, Broadway becomes exciting. Colorful traffic. Beautiful shop windows. Huge multicolored posters and signs advertise everything from plays and movies to Camel cigarettes. There is a billboard that I can't stop staring at. It's a man in a Fedora whose mouth is open—and puffs of smoke blow from his parted lips! A sign that smokes! Tommy turns off Broadway toward the Empire State Building.

"I'll park somewhere near, and we'll walk to it."

The Empire State Building is a staggering sight. It seems to sway as I crane my neck to follow it to the top. As the clouds drift above, the building seems to swing in the direction opposite to that of the clouds. The thrill reverberates in my body, makes my stomach churn.

Oh, Papa, it has come to pass. The "cloud scraper" is just as exciting as you promised. The shops on Broadway are just as glamorous. But, Papa, where are you? You promised to stroll with me on Broadway, to buy me the prettiest dress. I stand here at the foot of the Empire State Building, the tallest building in the city of your dreams, and the mass grave in Bergen-Belsen casts an enormous shadow over it all. And for a moment the excitement turns to ashes in my mouth.

But I will not let the mass grave be the final arbiter of your dreams! Your dreams are not buried in Bergen-Belsen. I will make them live on here in New York. I will make all your dreams live on. I promise I will make all your dreams come true.

Chapter Four

ARE FAIRY TALES REAL?

Today at 11:00 A.M. Mother and I have an appointment at the offices of HIAS to meet our social worker. Aunt Celia, who works in a tie factory, where she stitches cotton lining into silk ties, takes the day off to accompany us on the Brighton train to Manhattan, where our meeting with the social worker is to take place.

The trip gives Celia a chance to teach us how to travel on the subway, how to purchase a token for a nickel at the booth and slip it into a slot in the turnstile, how to pass through as you turn the arms of the turnstile.

She directs a warning to Mommy: "Be careful not to miss your turn to pass through. If you miss your turn you'll lose your nickel, you'll have to buy a new token and start all over again." Seeing Mommy's panic-stricken face, Celia adds encouragingly, "Don't worry, Laurika, you'll make it. Just watch me. I'll go through first."

Success! Both Mother and I manage the subway turnstile without a mishap. It's late morning and the Brighton

Local is empty; the three of us are the only passengers in the car for a while. As we approach Manhattan a number of other riders join us. The passengers enter, take their seats in total silence, staring directly ahead with blank faces, then leave just as they came, without a word. They don't greet us or each other upon entering, don't exchange a single word with any other rider, and don't say good-bye upon leaving. No one even exchanges glances with other subway riders. They behave as if they belonged to a secret society sworn to silence, or as if they considered each other enemy aliens. I wonder why.

"In Europe people talk to each other on trains. Here why doesn't anyone say hello as they sit down next to another passenger?" I ask Aunt Celia in a whisper.

"You don't have to whisper," Aunt Celia reminds me. "You can be sure no one here understands Hungarian. I also found it strange at first, no *hello*, no *good day*, no *good evening*, not only on the subway but also on buses and in shops. If you say hello or good day, they look at you as if you were insane. You learn fast. Now, two years later, I don't even remember that I have ever greeted anyone in a public place."

"It seems rather unfriendly. Are Americans unfriendly in general?"

"No, this is just part of the culture. You'll get used to it."

Mother is watching the women's clothes—what do they wear, what's the latest style?

"The skirts are much longer here," she remarks. "And the colors are rather dark. I see browns, grays, a lot of black. Amazing—I'd have thought it would be the other way around. Europe has the reputation for being conservative, not America!"

In about half an hour we reach our destination. The walk from the subway to HIAS takes about five minutes. Although we are a little early the receptionist ushers my mother and me directly into one of the offices and bids Aunt Celia to wait in the hallway.

"Laura and Elvira Friedman are here to see you."

A stocky, middle-age woman sits behind a massive mahogany desk.

"I'm Mrs. Ryder, your social worker," she says in a deep monotone voice as she rifles through the folders piled high on her desk.

I realize Mother and I are one of the folders on Mrs. Ryder's desk. Finally she locates the folder she was looking for and keeps perusing it while explaining the social worker's function, which is to serve as our liaison with HIAS, monitoring the various forms of assistance provided by HIAS, helping us find housing, employment, and medical care.

"Do you have any questions?"

"Yes. May I translate for my mother and see if she has any questions?"

Mrs. Ryder nods, and Mommy, after listening to my synopsis in Hungarian, exclaims, "Medical care? That's very good. We need to see a doctor about your persistent stomachache and lack of appetite."

"We have a list of physicians who have volunteered their services to HIAS," Mrs. Ryder responds. "Let's find a doctor in the proximity of your home. Here is one. He is Dr. Alexander Hirschfield, a family physician with a specialty in internal medicine. His office is on Thirteenth Avenue in Brooklyn. . . . Shouldn't be too far from where you live. Do you want me to make an appointment for you?" she asks as she picks up the telephone.

"Oh, certainly. Thank you. That would be extremely kind."

"Dr. Hirschfield can see you this afternoon at two o'clock." Mrs. Ryder covers the mouthpiece of the telephone with her hand. "Shall I make the appointment?"

I nod eagerly, and she jots down the information on a slip of paper.

Mother and I are overwhelmed with gratitude. I wish I could muster more elaborate thanks, but my English is rather limited. All I can say is "Thank you" once more.

"Thank you," Mother repeats as we walk out the door.

We get home in ample time for a bit of lunch. Luckily Aunt Celia has taken the day off; she can accompany me to the doctor. It's a complicated route with two buses to Thirteenth Avenue and Fiftieth Street, in the Borough Park section.

To my great distress we arrive almost half an hour late for the appointment. I feel acute embarrassment for not finding the right English words to apologize, to explain that I arrived only a few days ago and Aunt Celia must have miscalculated the length of time the bus ride would take . . . and the time of waiting for transfers. I do not notice that Dr. Alex Hirschfield is not listening to my apology.

Neither do I notice what Aunt Celia later describes as

"a strange, dreamy look in the doctor's eyes while he went through the motions of taking your history, as if in a fog," and "the foolish angelic smile that settled on his face after the medical exam!"

"A medical exam that lasted forever. He's moon-struck, the poor fellow!" Aunt Celia winks. Despite my vehement protestations, Aunt Celia keeps up her banter all the way home from the doctor's office, teasing me mercilessly about having "bewitched a perfectly nice doctor." And when we arrive home, Aunt Celia bursts into the apartment to announce to Mother and Uncle Martin that my medical diagnosis was fine but "the same cannot be said of the poor doctor who is hopelessly sick—lovesick."

"Nonsense!" I shout indignantly. "Dr. Hirschfield seems like a careful doctor, that's all. My ulcer's acting up, and he's sending me for some tests. What should he do—ignore a bleeding ulcer? In Munich I was hospitalized for months with my ulcer!" But nothing I say seems to have an effect on the three of them; they keep up their relent-less teasing.

In the evening the phone rings, and Celia's voice is rippling with glee as she announces, "Elli. It's for you. It's Dr. Hirschfield!"

"Didn't I tell you? Is he moonstruck or what?" Celia gloats when I hang up.

"What's so amusing?" I demand to know. "The doctor phoned to ask about my health, and wants to see me in his office tomorrow. He has to set up all the necessary tests as soon as possible."

On Tuesday I no longer need Aunt Celia to accompany me to Dr. Hirschfield's office. As a matter of fact, I discover a shortcut and this time arrive ahead of my appointment.

A wide grin lights up the doctor's tan face when he spots me among the patients in the waiting room. "Ah, Miss Friedman, you made it on time!" he exclaims with palpable delight, and I notice a dimple in his left cheek. "Please come into the office."

Dr. Hirschfield's joy at seeing me seems totally uninhibited, like the joy of a child. His whole being seems to radiate a boundless capacity for joy. Like a radar, within seconds after entering the medical office I detect his vibes and get caught up in his excitement.

The medical consultation turns into an emotional encounter. Dr. Hirschfield wants to know "everything" about me, about my life, especially the history of my experiences during the Holocaust.

"In which concentration camp were you incarcerated?" he asks, and his deep blue eyes glisten with feeling. I can see compassion and pain reflected in them. And something else I cannot identify.

"First in Auschwitz, and then——"

"Auschwitz!" he interrupts, crying out. "Forgive me . . . but I've never before met anyone who had been in Auschwitz!" He takes my hand into his and his eyes overflow with tears. "My poor child. I want to tell you something I've never told anyone. I was born in Germany, and . . . both my father and my mother perished in Auschwitz. And you . . . you had been there . . . and came out of the inferno that consumed my parents. For me you are a messenger . . . my angel. *Meine engel*. I'll forever be grateful to HIAS for bringing you to me."

I don't know what to say. I am shaken to my core by the virtual onslaught of emotions . . . his and mine.

"I promise I'll make you well. I will take care of you as if you were my sister. I want to make up for all you've been through . . . if you let me." His eyes are pleading. "If you'll let me."

"Dr. Hirschfield . . ." Tears well up in my throat, choking me. I cannot breathe . . . I cannot utter another sound.

"Call me Alex, will you, Elli?"

I take a deep breath. "Yes," I croak, and a new barrage of tears threatens to drown out my words. "I'm happy to call you Alex. And I am very grateful. I must admit, I'm a bit frightened . . . afraid of America . . . a bit scared. There is so much I don't understand. I do need a friend. Thank you for offering—is *offering* the right word? Thank you for offering to be my friend."

"My poor child. I'll be happy to be your friend, Elli, if you let me. It would mean the world to me! My angel, I must go now. The patients are waiting. Here's a list of tests you'll need. I'll make the appointments for you and arrange my schedule so I can take you, be with you through it all."

"How soon will those tests be? You see, Doctor . . . I mean, Alex, the Jewish holiday of Passover is in ten or eleven days . . ."

"No problem. We can have them done after Passover.

In either case it takes time to line up all the tests. *Auf Wiedersehen, mein engel.* See you soon, my angel!"

Alex's embrace is energetic yet gentle and generous . . . and loving. The embrace of a friend—or of a father?

When he holds me close I feel like Cinderella in the arms of Prince Charming. Is Dr. Hirschfield my Prince Charming? Can it be? Can this be happening to me?

In America are fairy tales real?

Chapter Five

PASSOVER PREPARATIONS

"What perfect timing," Uncle Martin declares. "We will celebrate your arrival in America, the land of freedom, together with the holiday of Passover, the Festival of Freedom. What a wonderful coincidence!"

I am excited, and strangely moved, by the symbolism. Although Jewish tradition shuns omens, lists them as superstition and therefore forbidden, I confess I have always clung to a belief in coincidental occurrences as covert messages, and now cannot help but see in our arrival so close to the Jewish Festival of Freedom a good omen for our future in America.

But for the Jewish housewife the days before Passover ironically are days of slavery. Even before cooking and baking for the holiday, particularly for the main event, the Passover Seder, the entire house must be free of leavened bread and other food fragments. My mother's frantic cleaning campaigns before Passover made me dread the days before the holiday.

Now Aunt Celia is feverishly engaged in spring cleaning and myriad other preparations for the holiday. She gets home from work after six and immediately plunges into housework.

"Why don't you let us help out?" Mother raises the issue for the umpteenth time. "Elli and I feel so useless watching you do all the work. Why don't you assign some tasks for us to do?"

"No way!" Celia waves her arms in the air. "No way! You are guests in my home. You have not yet had time to recuperate from the arduous journey. You've only been here three days. Take it easy for a while. You'll have plenty of time to work later."

"Four days," Mother corrects her younger sister. "We have been here four days and have had enough rest. It's about time you let us help out," Mother protests, watching helplessly as Aunt Celia rolls up the small carpet in the foyer, carries it to the window, and, unrolling it on the windowsill, beats it with ferocious urgency, tennis racket in each hand. The bucket comes out next and soapy water is splashed on the linoleum floor, while Mother and I retreat to the sides so as not to be underfoot, to clear the arena for my aunt's mopping.

"But this is absurd!" Mother bursts out. "How can we stand by idly while you labor like the devil after a long day's work at the factory? You must let Elli and me share in the work."

"You don't know my house, don't know where things are, what has to be done and how. It's easier if I do it myself," Aunt Celia argues while the wet mop in her hands deftly spreads the suds all across the floor. "Why don't you relax on the couch in the living room until

Martin gets home. Then we'll have dinner. Maybe after dinner we'll discuss the issue of your helping out."

Mother, unaccustomed to obeying her younger sibling's orders, or anyone else's, for that matter, grumbles as she heads with reluctant strides to the living room, and I follow suit.

"Aunt Celia," I open the discussion after dinner in hopes of preempting Mother's potentially argumentative approach and preventing a confrontation between these two strong women. "We know that you want to make us feel welcome by freeing us from household chores. But still, you'd make us feel more welcome if you allowed us to help out."

"Well put!" Uncle applauds. "My dear niece, I believe you should opt for a diplomatic career. But all joking aside, Celia, why don't you assign some household chores for Laura and Elli if they want to help?"

My aunt relents. "Okay, you eager beavers. You can do the shopping for me. By the time I get home, most of the stores on Kings Highway are closed. That would really be a big help. I'll prepare a shopping list for groceries, bread, fruit, and vegetables and some household items. All the stores that you'll need are on this side of the highway, except the bakery. There's a Woolworth store beyond the subway station, there you'll find all kinds of things I'll include in the list, like thread for sewing, shoe polish, and toothpaste."

"Do you know all the English words for these?" Mother asks me after perusing the list Celia has made out in Hungarian.

I glance at the piece of paper. "I hope so. If not, I can find them in the dictionary."

From the broom closet Aunt Celia produces an aluminum contraption. "See? This is my shopping wagon. You open it like this and it can hold all your bags, fruit, vegetables, everything. You don't have to carry heavy packages in your hand."

My superpractical mother is fascinated with the shopping cart, especially with the way it folds into a flat object that is easily stored in a narrow space.

In the morning after Celia and Martin leave for work, Mother and I set out on our shopping expedition with a sense of high adventure. Our good mood must be contagious: On the street people smile and wave at us. At the fruit stands we are enthralled with the abundance of fruit and vegetables; in the grocery store, with the lavish display of foodstuffs, the virtual paradise of dairy products. Even basic staples like flour, sugar, and salt, in Europe measured out of large sacks into brown paper bags, here are packaged in small, colorful containers that are attractively arranged on open shelves!

At the bakery I learn a lesson for lifelong use. "If you want your bread and baked goods to remain nice and fresh," the baker explains, "never put them in the refrigerator. In the refrigerator baked goods turn stale. Instead put your bread and your cake in the freezer while they're still fresh. When you're ready to use them you'll find that they defrost very quickly, and are as fresh as the day they were baked."

Woolworth's, a five-and-ten store where you can buy

anything from a shoestring to a shopping cart, and where all small items cost either a nickel, five cents, or a dime, ten cents, is a newcomer's Mecca. We purchase a hair comb, cotton thread for sewing, needles, wool for knitting, toothpaste, shoe polish, soap, a small mirror, and a miniature sewing kit as a present for Aunt Celia.

Leaving Woolworth's our jolly mood receives a sudden blow: The shopping cart we parked in front of the store laden with all our purchases is gone! How can it be? Perhaps we left it in the adjacent doorway. It's not there. Perhaps someone rolled it into the store. We run to the store manager to inquire.

"Where did you leave your shopping wagon?" the store manager asks, incredulous. "Outside the store? On the street? What did you expect?"

What did we expect? We expected to find it where we left it. Just as it would have happened in all the European towns where we'd lived. One thing we did not expect: that this generous, openhearted country would have heartless thieves.

Instead of being upset over the heavy loss Mother and I have incurred, Aunt Celia, with her impromptu knack for humor, turns our disaster into a farce, easing our sense of guilt.

"Meet my family from Timbuktu!" she chuckles boisterously when she hears our sad story. "This is America, the land of limitless opportunity—even for incompetent thieves. You proved it today. You made some hapless thieves very happy today!"

"Being a newcomer is a learning experience," Uncle

says amiably. "You've just had your first lesson: Never leave your belongings unattended, not even for a second. I'm sorry you had to learn it this way, but consider it a tuition fee."

All the neighbors who hear about our experience echo Uncle's commiseration and repeat his advice. A number of the tenants in the building are new immigrants, and try to comfort us. They assure us that soon we'll earn enough money to repay the damage, even forget it ever happened.

"You'll soon forget the whole incident," one neighbor predicts.

"But remember the lesson you've learned from it," adds another.

For me there is a second lesson, one that has less to do with the loss of material possessions. It has to do with the loss of trust—a blow that strikes a chord somewhere deep within me. I did not expect to be betrayed in America, in the city of Papa's dreams.

Before Passover begins Alex calls to wish us a happy holiday. His voice, the warmth it radiates, lifts my spirits.

Passover is a happy holiday after all. Aunt Celia's house sparkles, the table is brilliantly set with newly purchased stainless steel cutlery and white Melmac dishes. Of all her silver objects only the antique candelabra was "brought from home," dug up from the cellar floor where it had been buried during the Nazi era.

The table is set for seven. Two guests join Uncle Martin, Aunt Celia, Mother, Bubi, and me for the Seder, Margit Fried and Miklos Benedict, both lone survivors.

Margit, Celia's "camp sister," and Miklos, a neighbor from "back home," have never met before, and my aunt has a secret agenda in inviting them.

"Wear your navy blue silk dress," she advises Margit. "The one with the white collar. You look very good in that dress. Miklos is eligible, and he likes good-looking women."

Margit, whose husband and son perished, each in another killing field, is wearing the blue silk dress and a polite, timid smile as she looks across the table at Miklos, whose wife and three children suffocated in the gas chamber in Auschwitz and who, painstakingly turned out in an immaculate white shirt and a checkered tie, is somewhat stiffly fiddling with his cutlery.

We all wear our holiday best, and the men look resplendent in their new white shirts Mother sewed on a borrowed Singer sewing machine, her contribution to the holiday preparations. My heart is like the new glass tumblers in front of us overflowing with sparkling red Tokay wine. It is filled to the brim. With a sense of bliss I look at my brother whom I had not seen for so many years. With pride I listen to his scholarly discourse on the Passover Haggadah, and with gratitude I remember Alex's friendship. How I wish he could have joined us tonight!

The delectable aroma of Aunt Celia's chicken soup mingled with that of roast turkey wafts in from the kitchen. Aunt Celia is an excellent cook, and the promise of dinner at her table stirs the company to sing the melodies of the Passover Haggadah with added vigor.

The Seder is a bittersweet event. We celebrate our freedom from ancient Egyptian slavery and remember our modern slavery in Germany. We sing aloud about the glory of miracles that saved us at the Red Sea and in the Sinai Desert, and weep silently about the agony of our losses in Auschwitz, in Dachau, and in the slave labor camps scattered about the face of Europe. As Margit and Miklos glance at each other across the table I can see in the reflection of their shared pain a spark born. And my heart throbs with gratitude for the miracle of survival. For the miracle of life.

Our first Passover Seder in America—it is a happy event after all.

It is a good omen after all.

Chapter Six

AMERICAN PEERS

One evening during Passover week we have a pleasant surprise. Aunt Lilly and Uncle Abish drop in unexpectedly for a short visit. We haven't seen each other since our arrival, and I'm delighted to see them again.

"I have regards for you from Aaron Klausner and from Mary Zimmerman," Uncle Abish announces. "They were happy to hear that you arrived safely."

"Aaron Klausner? Mary Zimmerman?" Mother and I ask in unison. "Who are they?"

"You don't know? They are our cousins. First cousins to Mordecai and me. Their families came here many years ago, years before the First World War."

I have never heard about Papa's cousins here in America. I am especially excited to learn that the Klausners have a daughter.

"She is about your age, and she would like to meet you," Aunt Lilly adds.

A cousin my age, and she wants to meet me? I am ecstatic. "When can we meet? And how?"

"I will telephone them and transmit your aunt's phone number. I'm sure Judy will call you."

Judy? Is that her name? It must be a nickname for Judith. I like it. Judy . . . it has a nice ring.

Aunt Lilly must have contacted the Klausner family right after her visit on Monday, because Tuesday morning bright and early I receive a phone call from Judy Klausner, my new cousin. She sounds just as excited about our meeting as I am.

"We would love to have you come to our house for a weekend," Judy says breathlessly. How about this coming weekend, Friday and Sabbath, the last days of Passover? Can you come?"

"Oh, thank you . . . thank you for your kind invitation," I reply with repressed excitement, somewhat awkwardly. "But I don't know. I must discuss it with my family. Where do you live, Judy?"

"In Williamsburg. It's a section of Brooklyn. Your aunt and uncle will explain to you where it is. I hope you can come."

"I hope so too. Thank you again for inviting me. I'll call back with the answer."

"How will you get there?" Mother asks when I hang up. "I hear Williamsburg is quite far from here."

In the evening there is a family consultation about Judy's invitation. Both Mommy and Aunt Celia feel it is too long a journey for me to undertake by myself, but Uncle Martin dismisses their fears. "Elli is a big girl. It's about time she started traveling on the trains. I will explain which subway train to take to the elevated line and where to change.

There's nothing to it. If you listen to these mother hens," he says turning to me, "you'll never leave the nest. This invitation is an ideal opportunity for you to test your independence."

Their resistance overcome, my two mothers start fussing over my clothes.

"What will you wear? You don't have any proper clothes," Mother declares.

"Yes indeed," Aunt Celia chimes in. "You can't go for a two-day visit to an American family wearing the dress you have. Your cousin Judy is an American girl. She probably has a different outfit for every day of the holiday."

"What's wrong with the dress she's wearing now?" Uncle asks indignantly. "It's colorful, it's clean, and it fits her well. With a figure like hers, she looks fabulous no matter what she wears."

"Thank you, Uncle, for sticking up for me. But be careful not to make my aunt jealous with your lavish compliments!"

Mother and I have no money to buy new clothes, no money at all. Uncle's intervention saves me from the embarrassment of having to admit it.

The phone rings. "It's your Uncle Abish. He wants to know if you are free tomorrow to go . . . but wait, he wants to talk to you."

Martin hands me the telephone receiver, and I cannot believe my ears when I hear what Uncle Abish called about. My heart dances with glee as I hang up.

"You won't believe this!" I shriek. "And don't say I've made this up! Do you know what Uncle Abish

54

wanted? Tomorrow they want to take me out to buy me a new summer outfit!"

All three of them cheer. "You'll end up making me into a believer in your mystic coincidences," Uncle Martin declares.

Uncle Abish and Aunt Lilly arrive in the afternoon in Tommy's convertible, and take Mommy and me to Union Square in Manhattan. Uncle parks the car in front of a building decorated by enormous blue letters— KLEIN'S DEPARTMENT STORE. What's a department store?

Soon I find out that a department store is an over-whelming experience. Noisy shoppers cluster around piles of merchandise on long tables, others peruse clothes on hangers arrayed on long metal rods, and still other shop-pers try on jackets and skirts in front of mirrors propped up among the aisles. And through all the shrill hustle and bustle cuts the insistent chiming of an invisible bell. All this cacophony combines to produce a hypnotic effect on me: I move about like a sleepwalker under a full moon.

At Aunt Lilly's urging I look through racks and racks of skirts and tops in a daze, dozens and dozens of them, of various shapes and colors while dodging the elbows of other shoppers.

"Can't you find anything you like?" Aunt Lilly asks cheerfully.

"What about this one," Mother suggests, yanking a pale blue outfit off the rack. "Try on the top to see if it fits." The two women pull the top over my head, right over the dress I am wearing, and drag me to the nearest mirror. I look like a stuffed, pale scarecrow ready to keel over.

"Beautiful!" Aunt Lilly exclaims. "It's perfect on you. You look great."

"Not bad," Mother concurs, and I am ready to pass out. Thank God the two women decide there is no need to try on the skirt; the skirt looks perfect.

"Oh, thank you. Thank you!" I shout, ready to head for the exit.

"Not yet, not yet," Uncle Abish warns. "I want you to pick out a jacket from among these. They're called coolie coats, the latest fashion rage."

The "latest fashion rage," flared jackets with flared sleeves, come in two colors: white and red. Mother opts for red, more practical, and once again I'm posed in front of a mirror to be admired by the two sisters-in-law. Now even Uncle Abish joins in the chorus of approval, and I have no choice but to graciously submit to majority opinion.

"Don't you see how striking you look? This red is fabulous—it's your color!" Aunt Lilly rhapsodizes.

"I must say it's quite becoming," Mother concurs once again. Thank God they all acquiesce, Uncle Abish takes the garments to the cashier, and I hug and kiss him out of gratitude for putting an end to my torment! The exit is near the cashier and we file out of the department store, lugging the packages that now help pave the way for my visit with the Klausners.

The view from the elevated train on the way to Williamsburg is enthralling. Entire neighborhoods unfold below my window as the subway car rattles unsteadily past.

My whole body is taut as a piano wire in observing the scene and watching for the names of the stations so as not to miss Penn Street, my stop. I note that the car doors slide open and shut in a matter of seconds. I pray silently that I succeed in slipping out of the train in time.

It's about an hour before sundown when I reach the Penn Street Station in Williamsburg and exit the train without mishap. Standing on the platform of the elevated train, I see that the streets of Williamsburg spreading out below me are alive with men of all ages scurrying in all directions, some wearing wide-rimmed black hats, others gray and brown fedoras, many others, black skullcaps. A distinctive air of the approaching *Shabbat* exudes from the crowd, and I am overcome by a sense of déjà vu. I have witnessed this scene. . . . I have been there. . . . I have been there long ago . . . in the vanished, never-never land of Before.

As I walk up the front stairs on Penn Street and ring the bell, I am gripped by momentary panic: What if these new cousins do not share my love of family? What if their invitation was a mere gesture of pity for a poor new immigrant?

But then the door opens, and all my fears are dispelled by the family's warm welcome. One by one they greet me in the narrow entrance hall. "*Isten hozott!* May God be blessed for bringing you here!" Judy's mother, Rozsi, cries out in Hungarian. Her embrace is followed by the embraces of her father, Aaron, and then Judy herself, and by the awkward handshake of her younger brother, Saul.

My sense of belonging deepens during the festive

Sabbath dinner. As we begin to get acquainted and the adults begin telling family stories, a new, magic world opens before me. I am amazed to learn from Cousin Aaron details of my father's family history I had never known! I learn how my grandfather as a young teen escaped from Czarist Russia, making his way west by skating on frozen rivers. . . . How he sneaked across the Austro-Hungarian border into Slovakia through snow-covered woods and made his way to the first major town where a wealthy grain merchant took him in and gave him shelter.

Mr. Weinstein, the kindhearted grain merchant of Bartfeld, or Bardejov as the town is called in Slovak, was known for helping the needy and sheltering fugitives from Czarist tyranny. He was known for providing them with money and supplies and helping them to continue their way to safer parts in the interior of the country.

In my grandfather's case, however, the relationship did not end there, Aaron relates. Mr. Moshe Weinstein recognized the athletic young man as a fine Hebrew scholar, and when he noticed a special attraction between him and his eldest daughter, Chava, he decided to arrange a marriage between the young couple.

"My grandmother Chava and grandfather Getsel! So Mr. Weinstein, the generous grain merchant, was Papa's grandfather! I've never heard any of this! Why didn't Papa tell me any of this?"

"He couldn't," Aaron explains. "In your country it was too dangerous to talk about your grandfather's escape from Russia, his illegal entry into Slovakia. All the children were sworn to secrecy. It is only here in America that it's safe to talk about it."

I'm fascinated by the encounter between my grandparents, between Getsel, the young Russian fugitive, and Chava, the rich man's daughter. Theirs was a fairy-tale romance, just like my encounter with Dr. Hirschfield. All at once they become real people, their story becomes real, and I understand the extent of my loss—the story I have just found is beyond my reach.

Grandfather Getsel died years before I was born. My grandmother Chava I met briefly when I was eight years old—for the first and the last time. The threat of war was in the air then; Hungarian forces had occupied our section of Slovakia, and one of Mommy's brothers came from Hungary through the newly opened border to see us. When he returned home he took me back with him for a visit in Hungary.

This brief spell of freedom was the eye of the hurricane, the beginning of the end. The end came rapidly. Five years later the family I met was no longer. Grandmother Chava together with her daughter and two youngest granddaughters suffocated in a gas chamber in Auschwitz. Her son-in-law and a grandson died somewhere in a slave labor camp in the Ukraine. And her two eldest granddaughters, whom I met briefly in Auschwitz, vanished in the vast gulag of German death camps.

During dinner I find out other amazing news. In 1905 Papa's grandparents Moshe and Sarah Weinstein left their five children and all their estate behind and moved to Jerusalem in the Holy Land! Papa's grandparents actually lived in Jerusalem and died in Jerusalem! And they were buried on the Mount of Olives!

"Wow! That's incredible news!" I exclaim. "Here I believed we had no roots . . . no ancestral graves anywhere! I believed all traces of our existence were wiped out by the Holocaust, and now I find out that Papa's grandparents are buried on the holiest site of the globe! Their tombs are to be found on the Mount of Olives! As soon as I can save enough money for a plane ticket," I vow, "I will fly to Israel to visit the graves of Papa's ancestors."

"Unfortunately you can't do that, Elli," Cousin Aaron says softly. "The Mount of Olives is Jordanian territory; it's off-limits to Jews."

"Since when?"

"About two years ago, when the State of Israel was established. The Arab states attacked from all sides, and the Jordanians succeeded in capturing East Jerusalem, the Western Wall, and many other Jewish holy sites like Rachel's Tomb in Bethlehem."

A deep silence descends on the festive table, and Aaron continues, his voice barely above a whisper, "News reached us that the cemetery on the Mount of Olives was desecrated. Most of the tombs were hurled down the slope, some used as steps for latrines, some carted away, to be used in highway construction. . . ."

What? The tombs of Papa's grandparents desecrated on the sacred Mount of Olives . . . used as steps for latrines! How could that have happened? And why?

I have just found them, Papa's ancestral graves. I can't lose them now!

"Don't worry, Elli," Rozsi interjects in a comforting tone. "The day will come when we will reclaim our ancestral graves, and we will restore them."

Judy changes the subject, and the mood shifts.

"My club will hold its weekly session here tonight," she confides, adding apologetically, "I could not reschedule it when I found out you'd be visiting. Elli, I hope you don't mind.

"Our meetings are held on Friday evenings in each other's homes," Judy goes on to explain. "It's sort of a debating society. For each session one of the members prepares a talk on a specific subject, and then the group debates it. Everyone is free to ask questions, make comments."

"Mind? Oh, no! I'm glad I happen to be here, to be part of it . . . to learn. What's the topic tonight?"

"Since it's Passover, the topic relates to the holiday. Tonight's the seventh day of Passover, the seventh day after the Exodus from Egypt, when the Children of Israel witnessed the splitting of the Red Sea and marched through on dry land. The lecturer will focus on the scientific debate that surrounds the biblical account of the miracle. The title he submitted for his talk is 'A Divine Miracle or a Natural Phenomenon?'"

How fascinating. I have never been exposed to anything like this. As the guests file in and the living room fills with girls and boys my age or a bit older, I feel my stomach muscles contract. How will Judy's friends relate to me? Will I, the greenhorn, be accepted by these young Americans, most of them college students? And I have not even gone to high school! Will they snub me for being younger, for my ignorance . . . for my foreign accent?

"Should I introduce you? Or you'd rather I don't?" Judy asks in a whisper before the room fills to the brim.

"No, no. Please don't introduce me," I whisper back.

About fifty or sixty young people crowd into the living room, the dining room, and the kitchen. They sit on every available place, and when even these are filled they sit on the carpet with natural ease, without a fuss. They fill the spaces between the kitchen and the foyer, and even the stairs leading to the bedrooms.

The lecture and the discussion that follows are even more interesting than I anticipated. The speaker poses a dilemma between the biblical account and the scientific approach to the splitting of the Red Sea, which formed an escape route for the Israelites from the advancing Egyptian cavalry.

"The biblical account is simple: It was a divine miracle. No explanation is necessary," the speaker begins. "The scientific approach, however, demands proof," he continues. "According to the scientific approach it was no miracle, but a simple natural phenomenon. A strong east wind, blowing all night, coincided with the ebbing tide and exposed the narrow isthmus joining the Bitter Lakes to the Red Sea, enabling the Israelites to cross as on dry land. How do you reconcile the two views?"

An animated debate follows, and I listen with growing amazement at the extent of knowledge and the depth of intellectual curiosity exhibited by this group of young people. How much I have missed! Will I ever be able to catch up?

I raise my hand to ask a question, and members of the group, one by one, turn around, curious to identify the unfamiliar voice.

"Meet my cousin Elli." Judy now rises to introduce me, and I feel like sinking into the ground. "She arrived from Europe two weeks ago. How do you like her English?"

"Almost three weeks ago," I mumble.

Some of the guests applaud, others offer friendly smiles, and I feel a surge of gratitude for the show of acceptance. The debate grows livelier as the hours slip by and the grandfather clock in the dining room begins to chime twelve.

"It's midnight!" Judy the hostess exclaims. "And I haven't even served you some drinks!"

She hurries to the kitchen and reemerges with a tray of fruit, cookies, and soft drinks, and the company cheerfully breaks for the refreshments.

As they leave, Judy's friends one by one shake hands, wishing me well in my new homeland. I am moved by their warmth and their openness.

Secretly I resolve to emulate these young Americans so I can become part of their world.

And one more thing. No one noticed the number on my arm. Thank you, God. Help me blend in.

After all the others leave, Judy's two close friends, Betty and Florence, stay behind a bit longer, and the three of us get acquainted.

"This was the best session ever," Betty says to me. "Thanks to your provocative questions."

"How do you like her English?" Judy asks again. "Isn't she something? She came just three weeks ago. Or not even?"

"We arrived on April seventh. What's today's date?"

"Today is the twenty-seventh," Florence offers. "A day less than three weeks."

The three of us laugh.

My voice drops as I make an admission. "I feel humbled . . . I feel humbled by this evening. This evening's session showed me how far behind I am . . . how very far behind all of you."

"Nonsense," Judy cries. "I tell you what's the difference between us—formal schooling. We are college students. All you have to do is enroll in college and you'll catch up in no time. Brooklyn College is not far from your aunt's house. We'll take you there, show you the ropes."

Enroll in college? How old do you have to be to enter college? They must think I'm much older; everyone does. How can I tell them I haven't gone to high school yet?

Judy and her friends promise to take me to Brooklyn College next Monday. They are determined to get permission for me to sit in their classes.

I'm thrilled. To be in a classroom once again! To sit in a college class!

Judy and her friends' promise is a secret treasure I carry away with me like a souvenir.

When I arrive back home the family gives me a hero's welcome, and I regale them with the news of my father's family history as well as with the session of the debating society.

"A notice came for an appointment with Mrs. Ryder on Monday," Mommy says later.

"Oh, no, not on Monday! On Monday Judy is taking me to Brooklyn College. When is the appointment?"

"Nine-thirty."

"That's good. I can still meet Judy and her friends at Brooklyn College in the afternoon."

At our meeting Mrs. Ryder gave us notice that we must regularly report on the progress of our job hunting and submit a receipt for every item we purchase. She warned that the money we receive from HIAS will depend on our ability to prove our need and will be repayable from our first earnings. But from her broad hints it was apparent that our allowance depended primarily on Mrs. Ryder's goodwill, and that this commodity was in meager supply.

At first Mother and I rejected the notion of accepting HIAS's allowance for living expenses. We were determined to make it on our own, without assistance from anyone. But when we discovered that our savings would not suffice even for basic necessities, let alone for setting up a household, and that these allowances were repayable from our first earnings in small installments, we consented.

Last week I bought a pair of shoes for six dollars. I carefully compared prices before I settled on the brown pumps in an outlet store for what I believed was a bargain price. I hate brown but chose it because it is practical. Mother pointed out that the shoe color must match everything you wear when all you have is that one pair of shoes, and I thought brown neutral enough to match most of my clothes.

I dread our meeting on Monday. I find it humiliating to have to produce receipts. Why isn't our word good enough?

As I hand the sales slip for the shoes to Mrs. Ryder, I'm confident that she will approve of my judicious choice. Mrs. Ryder peruses the slip of paper and her eyebrows shoot up in a menacing sign of displeasure.

"Six dollars for a pair of shoes?" Mrs. Ryder's voice cuts like a razor. "Didn't you know that you can get shoes for two dollars and ninety-nine cents?" Now she looks straight at me and her eyes are tiny thumbtacks pinning me like an insect against the wall. "Six dollars is much too extravagant for a pair of shoes."

"Tell her for two dollars and ninety-nine cents you can get only sandals," Mother says in Hungarian, and I translate. "These shoes are not only for summer but for the year around."

"In the autumn you can buy shoes from the money you will earn then," Mrs. Ryder snaps back, her voice retaining its fine cutting edge.

"What is she saying?" Mother asks. But before I can translate, Mrs. Ryder moves to the next item on our agenda. "And what about a job? When will you start earning your keep? HIAS cannot provide for you indefinitely."

When I translate, Mother waves three fingers in the air. "Tell her we arrived three weeks ago. And that included eight days of the Passover holiday. How can she expect us to find employment in such a short time?"

"HIAS is prepared to pay two dollars and ninety-nine cents for the shoes," Mrs. Ryder remarks while shuffling papers in our folder on her desk. "It's up to you to pay the difference. Now, let's see . . . I have a job offer here." She stabs her finger at one of the papers. "Buros Bags. The job requires no training, no language skills. You can start tomorrow morning." Now Mrs. Ryder raises her head from her folder and her piercing gaze probes the depth of my bowels. "By the end of the month you can start repaying what you owe us. In weekly installments."

"I was hoping to go to school," I say in a low, steady voice, my eyes meeting the challenge of the social worker's stare. "Could you help me find an evening job, so that I can go to school in the mornings?"

"In your situation the job comes first." She snaps the folder shut in a gesture of finality to underline her response. "Going to school can wait. It's a luxury you can't afford now. Maybe someday, once you have repaid us . . ." She picks up a piece of paper from her desk and hands it to me. "Here is the address of your workplace." On the sheet in block letters it says BUROS BAGS, COURTLAND STREET, BROOKLYN. "It's near the Manhattan Bridge, on the Brooklyn side. You can take the subway to a station near the bridge, and walk the rest of the way. Ask for the manager, Igor Polonski. Be there on time tomorrow morning at eight."

"What does the job entail?" I ask with a sickly feeling in my stomach.

"There is no job description here. What's the difference? It's open, so you can start right away. The sooner you start the sooner you'll begin earning money. And repaying your debt to HIAS."

Bubi had advised me not to start work immediately but to take time and acclimatize first. "Look around," he cautioned. "Learn what's out there. Find out what you want to do. Decide wisely. Once you start working you won't have time to make wise decisions about your life's goals."

But I have no choice. I must not antagonize Mrs. Ryder and jeopardize the HIAS allowance. We have no other resources. No money to live on.

Sitting on the bus on the way home I involuntarily hunch over my pocketbook, clasping it to my stomach. When will I continue my education if I have to take on a full-time job? Will I have to give up school altogether? How will my dream of becoming a teacher ever be realized? How about other job opportunities—will I miss out on those, as Bubi said? And the medical exams Alex has arranged for me? How will I manage to get to them? I should've told Mrs. Ryder about my medical tests!

Mother puts her arm about my shoulders. "Don't worry, Elli. This woman will not beat us. Remember, we have overcome greater troubles. This too we shall overcome."

Mother's reassuring words, as always, ease the pain in my stomach.

Suddenly I remember. "Mommy, do you know what today is? April thirtieth!"

"April thirtieth . . . ?"

"The day the American army liberated us!"

"Really? How could I have forgotten?"

"It was on a Monday—just like today."

"So you see, what better reminder does one need of what we've been through? And you see, with God's help we have made it. You'll see, *Leanyka*. Soon we won't need to kowtow to the likes of Mrs. Ryder. We'll earn enough to repay her organization. . . . And we'll be free . . . hold our head up high again."

In the afternoon as I make my way across the magnificent Brooklyn College campus to the library, where I am to meet Judy and her friends, my spirits soar as if the dreadful meeting with Mrs. Ryder has not happened. The guard at the gate directs me across a lush green lawn that reminds me of Vienna's Stadtpark.

The path that leads to the library is lined on both

sides with shrubbery and trees in glorious bloom. When I enter the library the murals on the walls strike me. I have not expected a school to look like this. The schools I have known were drab, no-nonsense buildings, surrounded by walls of stone, not greenery. Certainly the walls were not adorned with art.

"What a beautiful campus!" I exclaim with enthusiasm when Judy and her friends arrive. "And these murals, they are beautiful!"

My comments astonish the three girls.

"I've never noticed these things," Judy says. "I guess we've taken everything on the campus for granted."

"I've never noticed there were murals on the walls," Betty laughs.

As we leave the library building on our way to their class in Boylan Hall the girls insist they have gained a new appreciation for their college campus.

The classroom itself is also a source of revelation for me. I have never expected an atmosphere of such informality in a college classroom—the professor's leisurely presentation and the open, friendly interchange between him and the students who, by the way, are sitting on chairs that are not bolted to the floor!

After class Judy, Betty, and Florence have a short break and we go to the cafeteria in the basement of Boylan Hall. Over a cup of hot chocolate I tell my new friends about the meeting with Mrs. Ryder this morning and the disheartening news that school is not an option for me; I must take on a daytime job, starting tomorrow.

As it turns out, all three of them have jobs in the

morning and attend classes late afternoon and some evenings.

"You can go to night school," Judy advises. "It's no problem."

"What are the requirements for admission? Do I have to pass college entrance examinations?"

"No. All you need is your high school diploma, with average or better grades. I am sure you have better than passing grades."

"I have no grades."

"What do you mean?"

"I have no diploma. I did not go to high school. I did not even complete elementary school." My voice is barely audible as I say this. The three American girls are silent.

Then Florence says, "We must go to class. Let's talk about it after. There must be a way."

I must leave. Aunt Celia expects me home for dinner.

"Thank you. I enjoyed attending your class. It was a wonderful experience."

"Don't worry, Elli. We'll find a way," Judy says, and the other two nod agreement. "We'll make inquiries. There must be a solution."

What solution?

How will I ever gain admission to college without a high school diploma? And if I can't go to college, how will I become a teacher?

Chapter Eight

MY FIRST JOB

Despite my initial disappointment, I find myself anticipating the challenge of my new job with a growing sense of adventure. I wake up bright and early, and, armed with a sandwich and an ample supply of good advice provided by my "two mothers," I reach the Kings Highway train station even before 7:00 A.M.

Clutching the sheet of paper with the address of Buros Bags, I join a throng of people on the platform, awaiting the train. I stand at the edge of the platform to make sure I don't miss my train: I don't want to be late on my first day. The Brighton Express arrives, and a tidal wave of riders relentlessly sweeps me into the car. Wait! Wait! I'm losing my balance! I must hold on to something! I must hold on to something . . . someone . . . to regain my balance. The doors slide shut, the train picks up speed and is in rapid motion, and I have no room to pull myself into the right position. I'm unable to reach a strap. I am tossed back and forth, back and forth, as the train rushes on and on. *I have no room to move . . . to breathe . . . there's no air in the wagon . . . heavy bodies are pressing against me, bearing down . . . I'm suffocating . . . and the doors are shut tight. When will the doors open?*

When will the train stop?

All at once the train slows to a screeching halt and the doors slide open. Frantically I push my way through the crowd towards the exit, out to the platform. Thank God I've made it out of the wagon. I'm on an open platform. . . . I'm free.

There's a metal bench nearby; I sink onto its cool surface and take deep breaths. Thank God I can breathe now. There's air out here, unlike in the crowded wagon. Wagon? It's a subway car, not a wagon! Elli, pull yourself together, you're not there. You're here, in America, in the subway, not in the crowded cattle wagon destined for Auschwitz, for Plaszow . . . for Dachau. . . . The nightmare is over: You're on your way to work, in a subway car. In a subway car you're not locked in against your will. The doors open at every station, and you can get out . . .

Now I feel better, much better. I must continue my journey. The next train arrives with a frightful clatter, the doors open. There are only a few riders waiting to enter the car, and I manage to remain near the entrance. There's room here, and when the doors open air surges into the car. I am not trapped.

It's 7:40 A.M. when the Brighton Express deposits me at the De Kalb Avenue Station. I hope it's not too far from here to Courtland Street.

On the station platform a subway rider ponders. "Courtland Street? About a twenty-minute walk from here. Twenty-five, tops."

It is a quiet sunny morning, no people on the street. I walk briskly. Who knows if the man at the subway station did not underestimate the distance? I must make sure to be there by eight. I wonder what will my job be? Clerical? Secretarial? Bookkeeping? Mrs. Ryder is familiar with my qualifications. My typing is not great but I'm willing to learn. I can take dictation. Perhaps they will use my language skills for correspondence in foreign languages . . . or for answering the telephone. I hope my English is fluent enough for that. I hope my vocabulary is sufficiently sophisticated.

I walk the whole length of Courtland Street twice. It's ten to eight but I cannot see Buros Bags. I stop a passerby, and he points to a square, flat building at the bottom of a steep slope, in the vicinity of the East River. "See the large letters on that dark brown building, down there under the bridge—see BUROS BAGS?"

"Down there? Oh yes, I can see. Thank you."

The last words I shout over my shoulder as I skip down the slope. What is an office building doing in a godforsaken spot all the way down there on the riverbank?

Buros Bags is a low, barnlike edifice with the front door open. I stand in the open doorway searching in vain for a bell, so I knock on the open door. There is no answer. I knock again, louder. . . . Still no answer. What am I to do? Now it is eight o'clock. I can't afford to waste precious minutes on formalities. I take a deep breath and walk right in . . . and find myself in a huge depot partially plunged in shadows, with stacks of brown paper piled to the ceiling on all sides, as far as the eye can see. Stacks of brown paper and nothing else . . . no one else. Where's everybody?

"Hello?"

There is movement in the back of the space and a stocky man of medium height emerges from the shadows with stacks of shiny brown paper under his arms.

"Excuse me for troubling you, but I lost my way. The sign outside says Buros Bags but I'm looking for an office by that name. Can you direct me to the right place?

"Buros Bags here."

"Is this Buros Bags?"

"Buros Bags," the stocky man echoes in a voice as gray as the shadows, and turns to walk away.

"I'm looking for Mr. Igor Polonski," I blurt out, directing my despair at his broad back. "Can you direct me to him?"

The solid figure turns and fixes me with an indifferent gaze. "I'm Polonski." His black hair is slicked down, black eyes are set wide apart, each perching above a protruding, high cheekbone. His tone, in a thick Slavic accent—is it hostile or simply sullen? "What can I do for you?"

"I am sent by HIAS," I say. "You have a job opening?"

"HIAS," he echoes again, tonelessly. "Okay. Here." With a gesture of resignation the massive body named Polonski points to a wide counter partly obscured by the dark gloom against the nearest wall. "This is where you work."

I look around the bare depot. Where is everybody?

"Am I the only worker?"

"And me." Polonski answers impassively, and deposits the stacks of paper on the counter. "Here. You see this ream? See these markings on the counter? We make three sizes. See this cutter? To make small bag you—you move cutter to here. To make medium—here. And to make big bag—here. You understand?"

I take a deep breath and nod.

"After you cut paper you make fold like this." Polonski folds a brown sheet lengthwise, allowing one side to overlap by about an inch. "See?" Then, draping the stiff double sheet on his arm, he walks toward the shadowy back of the oblong barn. "Come."

I follow silently behind Polonski to the counter at the far end of the depot. By now my eyes have become accustomed to the dark and I can see the silhouette of a strange contraption. Polonski raises the lever of the strange contraption and slides the paper through an open gap. Then with a sudden lurch of his arm he brings the lever down, and I flinch. Raising the lever once again Polonski draws the paper out of the contraption, rearranges it so as to slide it in sideways, once again brings the lever down, repeating the operation one more time over the third side of the folded brown paper.

"See? Done. Sealed. Three sides. Now bag finished," Polonski declares somewhat more animatedly as he slaps the new brown paper bag on top of a stack of similar shapes piled high on the counter. "And your name?"

"Miss Friedman."

"Miss Friedman." Polonski seems fond of repeating me. "Come."

Now we proceed to another counter, another strange contraption, in another deep shadow. "You begin here, at cutter. First we make five hundred big bags. With this chalk here I mark big size on paper. Then, bring to cutter." Polonski slides the stack of huge, shiny brown sheets into the contraption, pulls the lever. The lever brings down the blade and . . . "Cut!" Polonsky grunts and I recoil, my finely honed sense of self-preservation automatically activated.

Polonski ignores my squeamishness. "Now you do it." He points to a thick stack of brown sheets on the counter. "That's fifty."

I reach for the batch of paper. I cannot pick it up but I cannot let Polonski see that the batch is too heavy for me. I brace my body against the counter and with determined effort manage to heave it on my arm and carry it to the cutting surface. Then, focusing with utmost care, I mark the size, place the batch under the blade, and thankfully the blade descends like a guillotine slashing the large ream to size.

"You start fold now, Friedmanova. Call me when you finished," Polonski declares, and disappears into the shadowy interior of the depot.

I fold and refold until a dull ache creeps into my lower back, and I have not yet managed to get the proper shape Polonski showed me. Just about an hour passes before I master the art of brown-paper-bag folding.

With a sudden start I become aware of Polonski's presence right behind me.

"Not finished? Why?" he asks dryly.

"It's . . . it was hard to do it the right way . . . at first. Now I know. I will work faster now."

Polonski places a hand on my shoulder. "Okay," he says, his tone at once amiable, his fingers lingering on my shoulder. Then Polonski removes his hand and returns to his counter in the back.

I work faster now. The dull ache in my back becomes more acute. And a new sensation, a feeling of unease, lodges in my stomach. What has brought it on? Was it Polonski's touch on my shoulder? His manner? All at once I realize that I am totally alone with Polonski in this isolated factory under the Manhattan Bridge.

My feeling of discomfort grows and beads of sweat gather on the back of my neck. Even before I finish folding the stack of fifty, I hear Polonski's footsteps, and a shiver passes down my spine.

"Not finished? I help you!" With a paternal gesture Polonski's arm now encircles both my shoulders. I can feel the warmth of his massive chest against my back. I can smell his moist, garlicky breath as it brushes my ear.

"No!" I scream in panic. "No. No help."

In a flash I push Polonski away from me, grab my purse, and dash toward the exit.

Once outdoors, I race up the slope, without turning, without looking back. I am out of breath when I reach the top, the safety of the busy street, and only then do I dare turn around. Thank God Polonski is not following. Yet I keep running until I reach the entrance of the subway station. I hastily slip the nickel into the slot of the turnstile, and skip down the stairs, two at a time, a scared rabbit. Even in the shelter of the subway's dank interior I keep listening for Polonski's footsteps, waiting for his massive bulk to emerge from the shadows. But the platform remains deserted until the train arrives, and within seconds I am safe behind the car's doors sliding shut.

It is only noon, and I am on my way home. My first day of work is over. Did I overreact? Was my panic justified? Polonski might have meant well. He might have had no ulterior motive in putting his arm about me. Perhaps he truly wanted to help. Have I misread his motives? Have I misjudged his intentions? Oh, my God, am I paranoid?

What will Mrs. Ryder say? What will everybody say?

Mother is surprised to see me return home so early. At first I hesitate to tell her the story. I begin by explaining the nature of the work at Buros Bags, the sheer physical exertion it required. The physical stamina I don't seem to have.

"Mommy, it was backbreaking work. I was supposed to cut and fold five hundred huge sheets. I barely managed fifty when I developed an acute pain in my lower back. I'll have to explain to Mrs. Ryder that I am not capable of doing such hard physical labor. I hope she'll understand, and find more suitable employment for me."

Finally I confess the true reason, and Mommy's eyes fill with alarm.

"You did the right thing, Elli. Without a doubt. There's no way of knowing what he was going to do next. Even if we give him the benefit of the doubt and believe he had no immoral intentions today, how long

LIVIA BITTON-JACKSON

would it take for him to take advantage of the situation—
all alone, all day, every day with a young girl in that godforsaken place? It's good you had your wits about you
and left that place immediately . . . in good time."

"What about Mrs. Ryder? How will I explain it to
her? By now Polonski must have reported that I ran
away. Will my word count against his? What if we lose the
allowance?"

"It doesn't make any difference. If she doesn't understand and cuts the HIAS allowance, we'll manage on our
own."

"Mommy, I'm sorry to be a failure. On my first day."

"Don't worry, *Leanyka,* you're not a failure. And we'll
manage somehow." Today, more than ever, I need her
affection. Her support. Her validation. "You are not a
failure. You did the right thing, no matter what anybody
says."

In the evening there is a call from Alex. How did he
know I needed to hear his voice?

"I have an appointment for you with a specialist, a
gastroenterologist, for tomorrow."

"Tomorrow? I don't know. . . ."

"Is there a problem?"

"Well, yes. There's a little problem. I must go see the
social worker at HIAS tomorrow." I break down under
Alex's barrage of questions and tell him the story of my
first day at Buros Bags. I also confess that I worry about
Mrs. Ryder's reaction.

"I must speak to her tomorrow first thing, give her
my side of the story."

"My poor angel. No problem—the doctor's appointment is in the afternoon. I'm free after two o'clock. I can pick you up after your meeting, and we'll talk about this. In the meantime I want you to know . . . I'm very proud of you," Alex says, and the compassion in his voice feels like a balm on my bruises.

"Thank you, Alex. Thank you for everything."

"Never mind, *mein engel*. See you tomorrow."

Chapter Nine

AM I IN LOVE?

Instead of scolding me, Mrs. Ryder is surprisingly sympathetic when I tell her what happened yesterday at Buros Bags. She immediately contacts the next employer on her list of job opportunities.

"Let me see. I think I've found something suitable. The Jewish National Fund, an organization engaged in land development and forestation in Israel," Mrs. Ryder explains. "They're looking for an office worker. The head office is in mid-Manhattan, twenty-one East Forty-First Street. I'll phone them and describe your qualifications. I hope you get the job. It shouldn't take you longer than twenty minutes to get there," she adds as she reaches for the telephone.

"Mrs. Ryder, I must keep a medical appointment today. Dr. Hirschfield is sending me to a stomach specialist. But if all goes well, I can start work tomorrow morning."

Mrs. Ryder makes the call, and the Jewish National Fund people agree to see me tomorrow.

To my surprise, Alex is waiting for me in the small lobby of the building.

"Dr. Hirschfield . . . Alex!"

"I thought I might as well pick you up from here. Dr. Fischler, the gastroenterologist, is actually nearer from here. And I thought in case you needed a support system I would talk to that social worker of yours. How did it go? Is everything okay?"

I nod, smiling. "Better than I expected. She was quite understanding."

Alex takes my arm and happily leads me out of the building to his car.

The gastroenterologist sends me for a GI series and Alex holds my hand throughout the battery of painful tests. And when the results show that I have a bleeding duodenal ulcer, he undertakes my treatment with such loving care I feel like a fairy princess in glass slippers.

Alex's nurturing, his ardor, is a warm glow for me to bask in, the promise of paradise. Seeing my happiness, in time my family's teasing changes to cautious, gradual acceptance of our relationship.

Am I in love? When did it happen? Did it happen when he fed me spoonfuls of vanilla ice cream to soothe the burning sensation in my stomach? Is it true love or am I moved by the tender touch of a father I have so sorely missed?

Or am I really just in love with my Cinderella role, with the heady notion that Dr. Alex Hirschfield chose me—an ungainly teenager with straight hair and buckteeth—as the object of his passion, his ardent courtship? Am I hopelessly in love with romance, with the fairy tale–like quality of our relationship—an affair between the humble young refugee who didn't even attend high school, the timid Holocaust survivor, and the mature, accomplished man of the world?

Alex is eighteen years older than I. During our long walks on the seashore I learn about his happy childhood in Düsseldorf, about his dreams of becoming a doctor in order to help ease human suffering. With a self-conscious chuckle Alex divulges that he was about to enter medical school the year I was born. But despite his being an outstanding student, his application was rejected because he was a Jew. Jewish students were not admitted to universities in his native Germany, and Alex's parents, both practicing physicians, sent their only child to study medicine in Italy.

And so it came about that Alex spent the war years in Rome, while his parents were detained in the Dachau concentration camp and from there deported to Auschwitz. When the war was over and he returned to Germany he found neither his parents nor his home: His parents were gone without a trace, and his home was taken over by strangers. In vain did he wait for their return, for news about them. . . . Until one day, a year later, his investigations yielded an answer: He found out that both his parents perished in the gas chambers in Auschwitz.

"You are my phoenix," Alex says, and tears glisten in his deep blue eyes. "My phoenix that rose from the ashes of Auschwitz—my parents' ashes. God sent you to me. From now on I will love God."

Alex becomes like a member of our family. Friday

evenings Alex joins us for dinner so he can learn about Sabbath observance. He watches Mother and Aunt Celia light Sabbath candles; Uncle Martin or Bubi recite the *kiddush*, the sanctification of the Sabbath with a blessing over wine, participates in the ritual of washing the hands before breaking the bread, and he is invariably moved to tears.

"I want to learn our faith," he reveals to me when we are alone. "I want to share your life."

Alex's desire to become a "good Jew" because of me deepens my attachment to him. It adds a spiritual dimension to our friendship.

"Don't let him get too deeply involved with you," Mommy warns when we are alone. "I don't mind him joining us for family dinners—he's a likable fellow, bright, intelligent, truly pleasant company—but you . . . I don't want you to get involved."

"What do you mean 'get involved'? He is a friend, that's all. What are you afraid of?"

"I'm afraid of complications. He's a much older man, and I can see you're impressed. I understand he's impressive but mainly because he's so much older, he's so much more accomplished than a boy closer to your age would be. I'd like you to go out with boys closer to your age—a year or two older—not like Alex Hirschfield."

"Mom, I'm happy with him. Is that what you are worried about? You don't want me to be happy? Is that the problem?"

Mother's eyes widen with shock. "What's the matter with you, Elli? How can you say a thing like that? All I want is your happiness. That's why I'm worried . . . as I watch this go on, you getting more and more involved with someone who is not right for you!" Mother's voice rises, becomes shrill. "And . . . Alex Hirschfield is not right for you, Elli. Do you understand? Do you? Elli, I don't want you to get hurt."

"Hurt? What hurt? He is a good friend, the best friend I ever had. That's all! Leave it up to me, Mom, to decide what's good for me. I'm old enough to know—"

"If you were old enough to know I wouldn't worry. All I'm asking, Elli, remember what I said. Bubi's also worried about you heading for . . . for complications. He's the one who'd asked me to speak to you."

Mommy doesn't say the words *falling in love*. In our family we don't use words like that; we use words like *complications*. But that's what she is afraid of. She's afraid that I'm falling in love with Alex, an older man who is "not right" for me. Why isn't he right for me when I'm so happy in his company?

Even Bubi doesn't understand? Even he doesn't care whether I'm happy?

Yesterday a postcard came from Stanko Vranich, my Yugoslav co-interpreter on the ship. It's a lovely, scenic view of Denver, Colorado. Stanko writes that he was sent there by NYANA, his sponsoring organization, to work as a bookkeeper in a technical college. He plans to come to New York for a visit during Christmas vacation, he writes, and hopes to see me.

I've hidden the postcard among my underwear. I don't want my family to read it, and start giving me lectures about boys my age. *Ha,* they would point out. *Here's a fellow who's right for you . . . the right age. Why don't you write back,* they would say, *and invite him over during his vacation? Spend time with someone your own age.*

My dear, loving family—mother, brother, uncle, aunt—can't I just be left in peace for once . . . to be happy? Without too much worry, too many discussions? Why can't you be like Papa's grandfather Moshe Weinstein, the kindly grain merchant of Bardejov? Why can't you appreciate our feelings for each other regardless of the differences between us?

Papa, what would you advise me? Would you understand what I feel for Dr. Hirschfield? Would you approve of him?

Chapter Ten

TUNA FISH, MILK SHAKE, AND BAGELS AND LOX

The shop windows I pass on Fifth Avenue are the most beautiful, the most exciting I have ever seen! I remember some of the elegant stores I saw in Budapest, or in Vienna and Munich, but none of them rival New York's Fifth Avenue. What a shame I have no time to linger and admire the fascinating displays of fashion, glassware, jewelry, and china. I must hurry so as not to be late for my new job interview.

Twenty-one East Forty-First Street is a very tall building. I am craning my neck to look up and count how many floors it has, but I can't see the top. When I enter, I am overwhelmed by the enormous lobby and the rapid flow of men and women crisscrossing the wide-open space, men in well-cut business suits and wide-brimmed hats, women in high heels, tight skirts, and frilly blouses, all dashing into elevators and vanishing behind sliding doors.

Clutching the slip of paper with the block letters MR. EPSTEIN, JEWISH NATIONAL FUND, 21 E. 41ST STREET, 28TH

FLOOR, I step into the dizzying current of human traffic and allow myself to be swept into an elevator. Seeing my companions press buttons on a panel, I follow suit and press the button for the twenty-eighth floor, and watch it light up.

My stomach heaves as the elevator lurches upward and hoists us into the heights without stopping. As we rise rapidly toward the heavens, all faces in the compartment focus on an invisible point directly above the door.

All at once the elevator comes to a halt with a jolt and the doors open. It's the twentieth floor. Most passengers exit from the elevator. Will the elevator stop on the twenty-eighth? Or will it rush upward again for twenty more flights? Perhaps I should get out here and climb the stairs to the twenty-eighth floor? I wonder: Are there stairs in this building? Before I have a chance to decide, the doors close and we are rising rapidly again. Before I know it the elevator stops again and the doors open. It's the twenty-eighth floor.

Mr. Epstein, a tall, gangly man rises from his seat behind a massive desk and greets me with a friendly, boyish smile. He has freckles and flaming red hair. Good omen. I'm lucky with redheads. I have a secret premonition I'll get this job.

"Sit. Sit. So you're with HIAS?"

"Well, yes. HIAS is my sponsor. I'm new—I mean, a new immigrant. Came twenty-five days ago."

"Oh, wow! That is new. Can you type?"

"A little."

"How is your English spelling?"

"Mostly okay. There are words I have to look up in the dictionary."

"Don't we all! We have dictionaries here. Can you do bookkeeping?"

"I can learn."

"Mrs. Kline!" Mr. Epstein calls on the intercom. "Come in please."

When Mrs. Kline appears in the doorway, Mr. Epstein unfolds his tall frame from his seat and, standing erect, ushers me toward her with a fatherly gesture.

"Take this young lady to Miss Sokol in bookkeeping. She'll be working with us." Mr. Epstein extends his hand. "Much luck, Miss . . . ?"

"Friedman."

"Much luck, Miss Friedman."

"Thank you, Mr. Epstein."

Just like that, I've been hired. I can't believe it. I can't believe it! In a matter of minutes I have a new job . . . in a new, beautiful place . . . in a beautiful new world. My hunch—the omen—proved right.

Two days ago all seemed lost. I was alone in a dark, dreary depot deep under the Manhattan Bridge, harassed by a baleful figure among stacks of brown paper. Today I am on the twenty-eighth floor of a splendid building . . . on top of the world. Instead of folding interminable paper bags in a Brooklyn basement, I will do clerical work in the pulsating heart of Manhattan. Thank you, God, for raising me up from the sinister to the sublime.

Mrs. Kline leads the way along the polished corridor to the offices of the bookkeeping department and conveys me into the formidable presence of Miss Sokol, the head bookkeeper. Miss Sokol's huge frame seems to form a harmonious unit with her large desk, and the two together dominate the room, dwarfing three smaller desks that are lined up alongside the wall.

Before rattling off my responsibilities Miss Sokol briefly introduces the occupants of the small desks, my future coworkers—Sally, a tall, statuesque brunette, and Evelyn, a rather slim, petite blonde. Sally and Evelyn watch with curious, friendly glances as Miss Sokol explains the system: how to enter into the appropriate columns sums of money that reach the Jewish National Fund from various sources; how to type headings on letters and addresses on envelopes.

"Your job also entails doing Tree Certificates," Miss Sokol intones with an obvious sense of self-importance.

When I inquire about what Tree Certificates are, Miss Sokol launches with gusto into a long discourse on the subject.

"Donations come in for planting trees in all parts of Israel," she explains with pathos. "People plant trees to commemorate various occasions—to honor friends and relatives during their lifetime and memorialize them after they have passed on. There are graduations, engagements, weddings, births, and demises." On *demises* Miss Sokol's voice rises with glee, and I shudder, wondering if demises are good business. But Miss Sokol continues her performance with bravado. "For every tree donated we issue a certificate. Here. This is how the certificates look." Miss Sokol dramatically pulls open her desk drawer and triumphantly shoves a glossy page in my face. "See?" All at once I notice that Miss Sokol's performance generates great amusement for the two young women at their desks. Sally mimics her gestures behind her back, and Evelyn's face is bright red from efforts to keep a snigger under control. "It's your responsibility to type the name of the donor and honoree on the Tree Certificate, preceded by the words *In Honor Of* when the donation is made in celebration of a life-cycle event, and by the words *In Memory Of* when the donation is made in commemoration of a demise," Miss Sokol concludes, once again intoning the last word with a gleeful flourish.

Sally and Evelyn become my close friends. The three of us form a solid front against imperious Miss Sokol. Sharing conspiratorial glances with each other behind her back helps us tolerate Miss Sokol's self-importance.

During the noon break the two girls introduce me to an American institution—the soda fountain. The soda fountain is at a counter in a drugstore nearby where Evelyn and Sally regularly eat their lunch: tuna sandwiches and milk shakes.

"What's tuna?" I ask, intrigued by the pleasant, unfamiliar fragrance.

"You've never eaten tuna? How can that be?"When I explain to them that I have arrived in America a little more than three weeks ago, the girls are aghast. They knew I was from Europe but assumed I have lived here for years. Both admit that I am the first "greenhorn" they have ever met.

"So what's tuna? It smells very nice."

Evelyn offers a bite of her sandwich, but I decline.

"Why not? It's delicious," she says. "Try it. I'm sure you'll like it."

"I eat only kosher," I explain, somewhat diffidently.

"But tuna is a fish. You can eat it."

"A fish? But it smells a little like liverwurst. Is it a kosher fish? Some species of fish aren't kosher, you know."

"Tuna is," Sally interjects. "I keep kosher too."

"Me too," Evelyn confesses in a low voice. "Why don't you try a tiny bit?"

Finally convinced, I take a small bite of Evelyn's tuna sandwich, and it's love at first bite. It's a dramatic moment—the onset of my lifelong infatuation with tuna.

And I notice that my new friends are drinking a foaming, cream-colored liquid in tall glasses with colorful straws. It looks intriguing.

"What's that?" I ask the girls.

"A milk shake."

"What's a milk shake?" I ask, and we all burst out laughing.

Once again the girls persuade me to take a sip of their milk shakes, and once again I fall head over heels in love.

For years tuna sandwiches and milk shakes constitute my dream lunch. However, for the time being I cannot afford the cost. Instead I happily munch on a hard-boiled egg and an apple I bring from home.

I am grateful to Sally and Evelyn for not embarrassing me by offering to treat me to lunch even after they find out how much I like tuna sandwiches and milk shakes. I know that the day is not far off when I also will be able to splurge on these delicacies.

This is what I love about America! The knowledge of possibilities and the freedom to achieve, if only I work hard. And I know I can work hard. I'll work hard to make money so Mommy should not have to worry about all the expenses. I'll study hard to get my high school and then my college diploma, so Papa would be proud of me. . . .

I love the marvelous personal sense of liberty generated by so many things people here seem to take for granted. Americans don't seem to realize all the glorious freedoms they enjoy, unheard of in other parts of the world.

Alex, who has traveled in different parts, likes to point out to me all the good things in American life in comparison to other places in the world.

"Do you know that here you don't have to carry identification papers, ever? There are no ID cards in America!"

"How can that be?" I marvel. "Everywhere I lived, without exception, you had to have identity papers on you at all times."

"Not in America!"

"But how do they check your identity?" I ask.

"Why would anyone want to check your identity? Unless you've committed a crime."

"And how do you prove who you are?"

"Why would you need to prove who you are?

Whoever asks who you are, give your name, your address, whatever. . . . Isn't that enough? If you drive, you have a driver's license. If you travel abroad, you have a passport. If you go to court, you bring along your birth certificate. That covers it. Why be bothered with ID cards? We are not a police state."

Alex's answers astonish me and make me think. Indeed, what's the purpose of a personal ID other than to make you feel suspect? Controlled. Here you give your name and address—that's it. You are an individual, trustworthy, proud. No need to prove. No ID cards. This is true freedom.

"Here you can open a business without a license," Alex adds. "All you need is money to rent a locality, buy merchandise, and you are in business!"

I can't believe it. No business license? In my birthplace first you have to do an apprenticeship, pass a certification exam as an apprentice, and only then, with proof of your qualifications to run the particular shop, are you free to apply for a business license. And then wait months for approval. It may take a long time and a lot of money until your permit is issued. And only then can you open a shop. My father, besides having to renew his business license every year, had to have it regularly inspected together with our business premises, incurring additional expenses. The police would routinely find a violation of some kind and suspend my father's license. And the process of having it reinstated would take time and money and more money.

I can't believe that in America you don't need a

license. How amazingly simple! How wonderful. You pay the rent, you pay for the merchandise; that's all it takes.

When Mother and I are told by our social worker at HIAS that we must have the translation of our birth certificates notarized, I ask Alex about a lawyer qualified to do notarization.

"A lawyer? What for?" he asks. "You don't need a lawyer. You just walk into a drugstore, and for a quarter you can have any document notarized, right on the spot."

"You can't be serious! For a quarter! Is the druggist qualified?"

"Yes, most druggists are notaries public. Take your birth certificates and the translation to the pharmacy near you—there's one on the corner of Kings Highway and Ocean Avenue—and the man behind the counter will affix his stamp and signature."

That's all? No questions asked?

"Later on, when you have a bank account in the local bank, you will be able to get your documents notarized there for free."

"Anytime? No quarter? Free?"

Free, what a beautiful word.

The sense of freedom permeates every sphere of life. Even in social contact: Instead of the intimidating Mr. So-and-So or Mrs. So-and-So, acquaintances are addressed by their first names. Even children call adults, among them parents of their friends, Judy or Bill. In Hungary, when addressing an adult, even *Mr.* and *Mrs.* are not considered sufficiently polite; children must add the word *Uncle* or *Aunt* to the family name, and even in casual conversation neighbors employ honorifics like *eminent madam* and *eminent sir.*

"Here it is customary even for repairmen, bank clerks, bus drivers, housemaids, to use first names in their relationships with their customers and employers. Here employees address the boss as Jim or Jack or Tom," Alex elaborates.

"Really? I just can't fathom such a thing. I can't even imagine calling superiors by their first name. Thank you, Alex, for pointing these things out. I have much to learn."

"And I'm happy to be your tutor, any time!" Alex replies with a wink.

Later in the day a humorous episode results from my pitiful ignorance. I'm alone in the house when the doorbell rings. An Electrolux salesman stands in the doorway.

"Thank you," I tell him before he starts his sales pitch. "We are not interested in a vacuum cleaner." I am about to close the door but something in the man's ingratiating smile, a touch of defenselessness, compels me to explain apologetically, "You see, we have no carpet."

"But this machine is different. You don't need a carpet. You can use it for many other things." His eagerness is compelling, and I still keep the door ajar. "If you give me just ten minutes, I'll show you. You've never seen anything like the special features of this vacuum cleaner."

I open the door wider and the vacuum-cleaner salesman lugs his machine and a carton of accessories across the foyer into the living room.

"Thank you, ma'am, for letting me come in," he says. "It's been a long day. Do you mind if I sit while I explain the various accessory parts?"

"Not at all," I say, dragging one of the dining room chairs into the living room. "Make yourself comfortable. Do you want a drink? You must be parched, talking all day."

"Oh, thank you, ma'am. A glass of water would be appreciated."

When I bring in a tall tumbler of cold water and hand it to him, the salesman's appreciation is heartwarming. "God bless you for your kind heart," he says with genuine gratitude.

After explaining the various attachments, the salesman prepares to demonstrate their uses. Pausing in front of the bookcase in the anteroom, he exclaims: "Books! Great! Let me show how this machine cleans books, virtually sucks dust out of them." And with that he deftly adjusts a small attachment to the hose and reaches to the top of a row of books on one of the shelves.

"What letters are those?" he asks, pointing to the gold-embossed characters on a volume of the Pentateuch. "Are they Greek? Is this the original New Testament?"

"No. They are Hebrew letters," I answer. "This is the Hebrew Bible."

"Hebrew?" The salesman is surprised. "Are you Jewish? How . . . how very nice!" he cries, searching to add something to prove his familiarity with Jewishness. "You know, I love bagels and lox," the Electrolux man insinuates, as if making a confidential revelation.

Bagels and Lox? I've never heard those two names before. I believe they must be Jewish candidates running for some municipal office. I feel sympathy for the salesman, who in his attempt to make a sale feels compelled to declare his support for these Jewish politicians I don't even know. I hasten to reassure him.

"Bagels and Lox? Who are they? I've never even heard of them."

Now the salesman virtually explodes with laughter, slapping his knees. "God, are you funny! Bagels and Lox, who are they! What a funny girl! Miss, you're funnier than Lucille Ball. . . . Boy, this is the funniest thing I ever heard!"

I am puzzled by his laughter. When the salesman's demonstration is finally over, I ask for his business card and promise to give him a call if and when Mother and I would be ready to invest $125 in a vacuum cleaner.

I must speak to Alex about this. I must ask him about Bagels and Lox and find out what's so funny about them.

Chapter Eleven

PICNIC IN THE LIVING ROOM

I manage to reach Alex in his office with my puzzling question.

"Alex, can you tell me who are Bagels and Lox?"

"Bagels and Lox?" Alex's tone rises in amused puzzlement. "Angel, the question is what, not who!" Alex laughs. "A bagel is a hard bun, a stiff bread roll, and lox is fish. Salted smoked salmon!"

"A bread roll and fish? Oh, God, now I know why the salesman was hysterical!" I tell Alex the story about the Electrolux agent. "But I still don't understand why did he try to impress me with the fact that he loved bagels and lox after he saw the Hebrew books on the shelves and discovered I was Jewish?"

"Bagels and lox are considered Jewish ethnic food," Alex explains, laughing even harder. "Actually bagels are from Russia, and lox from Norway, but it was Russian Jewish immigrants who introduced them in America."

"I have never seen a bagel or lox. How do they taste?"

"It's an acquired taste. The bagel is much too hard and chewy, and lox tastes a bit raw, salty."

"Also, Alex, one more question. Who is Lucille Ball?"

"She is a comedienne, who has a nightly show on television. Why do you ask?"

"The salesman said I was funnier than Lucille Ball."

"That's high praise," Alex chuckles.

"The bad news is I didn't try to be funny. . . ."

Now Alex is laughing almost as hard as the salesman did.

For days now New York has been engulfed by oppressive heat and humidity; torrid air pockets stubbornly lurk in all the nooks and crannies of Ocean Avenue.

"Why don't we go to the beach on Sunday?" Alex suggests.

"The beach! Alex, what an excellent idea!" I exclaim. "I love the ocean. And I love to swim."

"It's too early to swim in the ocean. The water is cold despite the heat, but I thought of a picnic in the park alongside the seashore," Alex goes on. "I'm thinking of the whole family. . . . Your mother, your brother, Aunt Celia and Uncle Martin—a family outing on Brighton Beach. It could be great fun."

Poor Alex. He loves my family. He has no idea about the battles I'm waging to save our relationship. As a matter of fact, they love him, too. They just don't want me to love him!

"A picnic in the park! Why not? Why not?" Aunt Celia echoes Uncle Martin's enthusiasm.

"What a shame Bubi cannot join us," Mother laments.

Bubi can't spare the time. He is studying for ordination.

I am so proud of my brother. Last June he received his B.A. degree, graduating summa cum laude, and this June he is to receive his rabbinical degree from Yeshiva University, no doubt with top honors.

On Sunday, noon, when Alex arrives and we load picnic baskets, tablecloths, jugs of lemonade, blankets, and even bottles of mosquito repellent in his spacious car, our sense of fun reaches a high pitch. We are about to leave when Mother excuses herself.

"You know, children, I'd prefer to stay home and have a rest," she says quietly. "I'm a bit tired today. Must be the heat."

We look at one another, at a loss for what to do. But Mother insists we do not change our plans. "You must go ahead with the picnic," she urges. "I'll feel much better knowing you're out there having some fun."

Alex calls me aside.

"Your mother looks extremely pale. Would she agree to be examined by me?"

It takes some coaxing, but finally Mother yields to family pressure and consents that instead of the beach Alex drive us all to his medical office. Nonetheless she keeps fretting all along the way to Borough Park. "I hate to break up the beach party. You've all been looking forward to it. . . ."

"And now we are looking forward to seeing you get well," Celia interjects.

Alex ushers us into the living room of his compact, well-designed home, which functions as his office. Celia and Martin admire Alex's paintings that hang on the walls; Uncle Martin is especially fascinated by a huge mural depicting the Fall of Satan, with Satan's countenance radiating regret and delight in equal measures.

"Whose work is this? I can't make out the signature."

"All the paintings seem to be done by the same artist," Aunt Celia observes.

"Alex. He paints. He's done them all. Isn't he good?" I declare proudly.

"I'm impressed. The man has talent. You told me he composed music. You never mentioned his painting!"

Mother emerges from the examination room with a smile. During the examination Alex must have entertained her with anecdotes, a heady mix of humor and nostalgia in *Hochdeutsch,* the German dialect with which Mother is familiar.

Alex calls me into the examination room. Carefully closing the door behind him, he confides in a tone of urgency, "The physical revealed a large abdominal tumor. Your mother needs immediate surgery. The tumor must be removed as soon as possible. If you wish I'll make arrangements for the operation, or if you wish, for a second opinion. Please discuss it with your brother. And, of course, with Mrs. Friedman. She might be afraid of surgery. I'll be happy to talk to her, to explain the nature of the problem. The nature of the operation. I will reassure her."

"Thank you, Alex." The tremor in my voice reverberates through my body.

"Don't worry, angel." Alex puts an arm about me. "Please don't worry. I'll be with you all the way. I'll do everything in my power to make it less difficult for you.

Your mother will be in good hands. I'll see to that. In the meantime I've told her I felt something in her abdomen and we'll need to do some tests. I believe it's best not to tell her too much at once."

Alex's reassuring attitude puts Mother, Celia, and Martin in an upbeat mood, and Celia issues an impromptu invitation to Alex for a picnic in her living room.

"What else do you propose to do with all this food?" Aunt Celia queries. Alex accepts the invitation and drives us home, where Uncle quickly spreads blankets and tablecloths, and Aunt Celia arranges napkins and cups.

I lock myself in the bathroom to overcome the violent churning in my stomach. My God, what kind of growth is in Mommy's abdomen? Will she survive the operation? Will she be okay? Please help us, help us.

By the time I emerge from the bathroom, the four of them squat on the blanket, busily munching on the sandwiches and toasting each other with lemonade.

"All we need is music," Alex remarks. "'The Blue Danube.' Do you have a record player? I have some Strauss records in the car."

"Sorry." No record player. No radio. Soon. Soon I'll earn enough money from my job to buy all these luxuries.

Two days later Alex arrives with a present for Mother: a radio.

"It's not a simple radio. It's also an alarm clock. And one more thing." Alex's face radiates with the excitement of the surprise he is about to unveil. "A coffee machine!"

"A coffee machine?"

With a flourish Alex plugs in the radio, and from his doctor's bag produces a can of Maxwell House coffee. "Look, Frau Friedman. All you have to do is set the alarm clock to the time you want to wake up. Fill the machine with water, add the coffee, and as the alarm clock turns on, it turns a switch to start the coffee percolating. By the time you are ready with your morning toilette, your coffee is ready!"

We all applaud the clever gadget and, moved by Alex's thoughtfulness, Mother makes a solemn declaration. "Whenever and wherever you can arrange the operation, Herr Doctor," she says in German, with European formality. "I have complete confidence in your medical judgment."

"I am grateful for your vote of confidence, Frau Friedman," Alex responds in kind.

"Will you have coffee with us, Herr Doctor?"

"Of course, of course. Thank you kindly," Alex welcomes the invitation. Aunt Celia produces a tin of freshly baked apple strudel, and the whole family joins in to celebrate the new coffee machine.

On Monday Alex phones with good news: He has pulled myriad strings and succeeded in getting Mother's operation, a radical hysterectomy, scheduled for next Friday at the Beth Israel Hospital in Lower Manhattan.

"Your mom must be at the hospital on Thursday morning for admission and preparatory tests," Alex reminds me.

So it has come. In three days Mother will be hospitalized. God help us!

"Thank you, Alex. For all your kind efforts!" I breathe into the receiver.

"Don't worry, Angel. Your mom will be all right. You'll see."

"Oh, Alex!"

I phone Bubi at his dormitory room. He knows I cannot take time off from my new job, and Aunt Celia has used up her sick leave squiring us around after our arrival, so he offers to take a break from his studies to accompany Mother to the hospital.

Bubi arrives home Wednesday night, and I feel as if a heavy burden begins to lift from my soul.

Chapter Twelve

MOTHER'S OPERATION

Thursday I count the hours till the end of the day. Following Sally and Evelyn's directions, I reach Beth Israel Hospital in less than an hour. I find Mommy in a crowded ward, looking pale and frightened. Her face lights up as she sees me approach, carefully tiptoeing among the beds.

While I sit at the edge of her bed and we talk, a bit of color sneaks into her cheeks. We reminisce about other "hospital adventures"—her hernia operation in Bratislava years before the war, and my appendectomy in Komarom during the Hungarian occupation, and then long stretches of hospitalization in Munich after the war when Mommy virtually "lived" at my bedside. Then I tell Mommy about my coworkers, about some amusing happenings at the office, and I can see her spirits rise.

All at once we realize that the late afternoon has turned into night, and Mother urges me to go home.

"Mommy, let me stay a little longer."

"It's late, *Leanyka*. Please go now. The ride on the subway to Brooklyn may be dangerous at night."

How can I leave her? She looks so frail, so defenseless. When will I see her next? I must be at work tomorrow; I can't be here during the operation.

With a heavy heart I leave Mommy behind in the hospital ward packed with twenty-two other patients to whom she cannot speak, in the care of doctors and nurses who cannot understand her.

I toss and turn all night. Will Mom survive the operation? Will she recover? Will she undergo much pain?

Friday morning drags on and on. My stomach contracts into a tiny ball, and the nagging sensation interferes with my work. I can't wait for the telephone to ring. It's almost noon. Bubi promised to call from the hospital as soon as the operation is over. What keeps him from phoning?

The ringing of the telephone startles me like a gunshot. I fly out of my seat and grab the telephone with shaking hands. It's Bubi. Thank God the surgery is over, and Mother is back on the ward. She is still groggy from the anesthesia, but the doctor says the operation went well and she will be fine. With baited breath I wait to hear the answer to a question I'm afraid to ask. Then I hear Bubi say the words: "Dr. Hirschfeld—Alex—was here during the operation. The surgeon told Alex the tumor was benign. He wanted me to be the one to tell you."

I give a little shriek, and the girls in the office look up in alarm. "Oh! Thank God!" I make a supreme effort to compose myself and say to Bubi, sobbing, "I'm coming as soon as I can get away. I've already told them here I must leave early."

"I'll wait here until you arrive," Bubi promises.

Miss Sokol has a heart, and lets me leave at two o'clock. It's almost three o'clock when I emerge from the subway station at Union Square. From here I run at a gallop to the hospital. Bubi rises from his perch at the edge of the high hospital bed when I enter the long, narrow ward. Mother is lying perfectly still, her face like an alabaster mask, her beautiful features frozen into a lifeless repose. The only sign of life is a soft, intermittent moan.

"Don't worry, Elli. Mommy is still under the effect of anesthesia. Gradually she'll come out of it." Seeing my terrified face, Bubi adds, "Do you want me to stay?"

Bubi must leave now in order to reach the yeshiva in Washington Heights before Sabbath begins.

"Oh, no. You must hurry. How will you get to school on time . . . before *Shabbat*?"

"And how about you? How will *you* get home on time?"

"Aunt Celia gave me the address of a Mrs. Wellkowsky—or Wellkowitz. I have the name and address jotted down somewhere. She is a distant relation of Uncle Martin who lives somewhere in the neighborhood. I can sleep there. It doesn't look as if Mommy will come out of it soon. I guess I'll stay as long as I can, and then just walk to this lady's place for the night."

Shortly after Bubi leaves, Mother's moaning grows louder and she begins to vomit. I hold the bedpan under her chin. Poor Mommy: Her whole body heaves with every attack of nausea, and when the vomiting is over, her head falls back on her pillow, her eyes closed. I keep mopping her forehead with a wet washcloth, and the moaning softens.

All at once I notice a bright red stain appear on Mother's cover sheet above her lower abdomen. As I watch, the stain spreads rapidly, and to my horror the blood, like a small geyser, starts spurting through the white cloth.

What should I do? There's no one in sight. I spot a nurse at the far end of the ward heading for the exit. I race after her. "Please, quick! My mother is bleeding. Come, please . . ."

"I'll be right there," she answers and continues on her way out. I grab her arm. "You can't leave. You must come and help me. My mother's bleeding!"

The nurse gives me an icy stare. "Calm yourself, miss. Your mother had surgery this morning. Some bleeding is routine."

"This is not 'some bleeding.' Blood is spurting through the sheets!" Reluctantly the nurse changes course and follows me. When we reach Mother's bedside, the entire lower quadrant of her body is covered in blood.

"Just don't panic!" the nurse snaps in her stress. She runs for help. Within seconds a young intern appears with the nurse in tow and asks me to leave the room.

Two orderlies appear with a stretcher, and Mommy is wheeled away. "Where are you taking her?" I yell after them.

"To the operating room. For a minor procedure to stop the bleeding. She'll be right back. Wait here in the ward."

The procedure takes almost an hour, and when Mother is back in her bed, her face is ashen, even more masklike than before. Oh, please, God. Save her. Save her.

Hours pass before the intermittent vomiting and moaning stops, and Mommy opens her eyes. "You are still here," she says weekly. "Isn't it *Shabbat* yet? How will you get home?"

I put my hand on hers. "Oh, Mommy. Thank God you're awake. How do you feel?"

"Nauseous. It hurts . . ." She moves her hand feebly to her lower abdomen. "But I think I'm better." There is a large jug of grapefruit juice on her bed stand. I pour a glassful and bring it to her lips.

"Mommy, the nurses say you must drink a lot. Can you take a sip?"

I lift her head, and Mommy takes a few sips. Then closes her eyes again.

An orderly appears. "Miss, it's ten o'clock. You must leave the ward."

"How can I leave? My mother is very sick. I must take care of her. Sir, please let me stay."

"You can't stay. I'll be back in ten minutes. You must be gone by then."

Just then I notice that the bottle of the intravenous fluid is empty. My frantic search for a nurse takes me out of the ward to the nurses' station, until some twenty minutes later a new bottle is installed. Just then the orderly reappears and demands that I leave.

"I can't! Look, I just had the intravenous bottle changed. If I weren't here, my mother would be dead. I can't leave if there's nobody here to watch over her!"

"Look, miss, this is America. Here people can't just do what they want. There are rules here. You've got to leave this instant."

"I have nowhere to go. Do you want me to sleep on the street? Let me stay here. I will sleep on the floor next to my mother's bed so that if she needs me, I'll be right here."

"I'm calling the hospital security. If you don't leave willingly, you'll be thrown out by the police."

How fortunate that Mommy is asleep and is unaware of all this! She is moaning again, and beads of sweat appear on her forehead. She must be in pain. I run to the bathroom to wet the washcloth, and as I mop her face her moaning softens, and then stops. The cool washcloth must have soothed her pain.

The orderly appears with two policemen. "Miss, it's past midnight. What are you doing here in the hospital?"

"I have nowhere to go. I live in Brooklyn. There are no trains after midnight. Let me stay here with my mother. Please. I'll be as quiet as a mouse. I'm not bothering anybody."

"It's against the rules. We must escort you out of the hospital. Don't make us use force. Come along quietly."

"Don't you care that I'll have to sleep on the street?"

"We have our orders. Don't make us use force, miss."

I bend over Mommy's deathly still, deathly white face and kiss her forehead lightly. "Good night, Mommy. *Shabbat Shalom*."

"At seven in the morning you can be back here," one of the policemen reassures me.

"Thanks!" I hiss the word at him and hope that it conveys all I feel at the moment—anger, disappointment, contempt, and paralyzing fear. Oh, God, please let me see my mother alive tomorrow morning!

It is a warm, dark night. Even the air stands still. I am clutching the piece of paper with the unfamiliar address. Which way should I turn to find it? There is not a single soul I could ask. No passersby, no policemen.

At 2:00 A.M. I am still wandering helplessly on the deserted streets. Finally I reach a partially lit thoroughfare and almost trip over a body on the sidewalk. Oh, my God . . . there are several other bodies alongside the wall. Are they dead? Are they asleep? A stale smell of alcohol permeates the air. What's the name of this godforsaken street? In the dim light I manage to decipher the sign, THE BOWERY.

Where do I go from here? I turn the corner, peering at posters for guidance and . . . what kind of writing is this? Can these be Hebrew letters? I rise on my tiptoes and strain my eyes to make out the lettering in the semi-darkness. There is no mistake about it: They *are* Hebrew letters on a marquee. The letters spell out something in Yiddish . . . the title of a Yiddish play. This is the Yiddish theater! This must be Second Avenue, and this is the famous Second Avenue Yiddish Theater! A hint of home in the middle of the night here in a no-man's-land, reeking of booze and strewn with sleeping drunkards!

As if the Hebrew letters were my lucky charm, a mysterious omen, two policemen emerge from nowhere. They are no less surprised to see me, and when I show them my piece of paper with my contact's address, they helpfully direct me toward Avenue C.

Avenue C is plunged in total darkness. Without even a hint of illumination I cannot make out numbers on any house. Most of the houses appear to be walk-ups with bell handles in the middle of the doors. Ringing the bell is prohibited on the Sabbath. And besides, how could I ring Mrs. Wellkowitz's, or anyone's, bell at three o'clock in the morning?

I sit down on a stoop and wait. Time is passing in slow, reassuring spurts. I have always been a night owl. I love the mellow, reassuring stillness of absence—absence of light, of sound, of movement.

All at once I spot a star directly above. Was it only three weeks ago when, sitting on a stoop just like this one on the upper deck of SS *General Stuart,* I raised my eyes in search of a random star in the dark expanse of the sky just like this one. Suddenly I was startled by Captain McGregor's voice right behind me. "Never search for a star, Miss Friedman," he said. "Let it search for you!"

Has Captain McGregor's playful warning truly happened? Has Captain McGregor really happened? Has Dr. Alex Hirschfield? The weekend in Williamsburg . . . And Sally and Evelyn? And, for that matter, Mrs. Ryder . . . and Miss Sokol? Buros Bags and Polonski? Have they all happened? Or are these faces, these events, nothing but random molecules of the still, dark night?

Light is filtering through the clouds. Dawn makes a timid, tentative appearance. Let me wait a little longer. Let me wait here for the morning.

When the dim light of dawn brightens to a robust yellow, I rise from my stoop and begin to make my way back in the direction of Second Avenue. It is not yet six o'clock, still too early to ring Mrs. Wellkowitz's bell. It is time for me to find my way back to the hospital.

A body is stirring in the front garden. I had not noticed him in the dark. The sound of hoarse coughing shatters the silence, and a whiff of alcohol drifts in the air.

"Hey, miss." The body is erect now, and I shudder as he is walking toward me. "Do you have a cigarette?"

"Sorry," I answer, and begin to walk briskly.

"May I walk with you, miss? I don't know my way around here."

"Neither do I," I say, hoping to sound dismissive, but the drunk gives a hearty chuckle and matches my pace.

"Then we might as well walk together. A young miss like you needs an escort at this time of the night. Or is it day?"

As we walk, my genial "escort" relates his poignant story of unemployment in Pennsylvania, his futile hunt for a job in New York, his lack of funds. By the time we reach the hospital, my heart is heavy with his pain, his hopelessness. I wish I could help him. And as I bid him good-bye and good luck, I know that he knows, and he thanks me with an embarrassed chuckle.

Quietly, unobtrusively, I make my way to the hospital room. Even before I walk through the open door of the ward I can see Mother is fully awake. Thank God! As I approach her bed, her face lights up with a brilliant smile. Thank God the worst is over.

Mother spends ten days at Beth Israel Hospital, as her recovery is hampered by a recurring infection. She is back home, however, before Bubi's ordination at Yeshiva University, and fully recovered to attend the impressive ceremony.

It is a red-letter day . . . for so many reasons.

Chapter Thirteen

I AM THE DOCTOR'S ASSISTANT

On Sunday Alex is taking me to a performance of *The King and I*—my first Broadway show! For the occasion Mother sews a white blouse with ruffles and a long black skirt from pieces of fabric Aunt Celia has given her as a present.

"Stunning!" Alex exclaims when I open the door, and he virtually snatches me off my feet. "You look simply stunning! My compliments to you, Frau Friedman," Alex says to Mother. "You deserve double credit—for the beautiful outfit and for the beautiful daughter."

Mother acknowledges Alex's compliments with a wan smile. Poor Mommy. I sympathize with her predicament. Ever since her operation she is in a quandary about Alex, walking a tightrope between her true appreciation for Alex's help and her concern about my relationship with Alex—in short, "complications." I know Mother, being candid by nature, would love to show her gratitude effusively but worries about Alex misinterpreting it as an endorsement of our romance.

"Thank you, Herr Doctor, for both compliments," she

says formally. "May I reciprocate by offering you a slice of fresh *kuchen* before you leave?"

"I apologize, Frau Friedman." Alex returns Mother's formality with a courteous bow. "But I must decline. We are a bit behind schedule."

"Then accept this instead." Mother draws from the shelf a large box of Barton's chocolates and hands it to Alex. I had told Mom that Barton's were Alex's favorite chocolates, so as soon as she returned from the hospital she purchased a box of bonbons and has been waiting for the right moment to present it to him.

Alex's face lights up with childlike delight.

"Thank you Frau Friedman!" he exclaims, and happily clutching the chocolates under his arm ushers me out the door.

Before turning on the ignition Alex rummages in the car's glove compartment. "Where are they? Darn it . . . I must have left them at home. I bought you opera glasses for tonight. Let's make a quick detour to my house. I want you to have them tonight. Opera glasses are great fun."

In less than fifteen minutes we are approaching the square brick house on the corner of Fiftieth Street and Thirteenth Avenue. "What's going on there?" Alex cries in surprise when he notices a small crowd at the entrance of his house. He deftly parks the car and approaches them at a run.

"What's happened?"

"Oh, Doctor, Frankie fell off the swing and is bleeding from his head." The mother moves closer with the sobbing little boy, his head wrapped in a towel. "Thank the Lord you're here!"

"We came here first," the father explains excitedly. "Before taking him to the emergency room at the hospital, just on the off chance that we might find you in."

Alex casts an apologetic glance in my direction, and unlocking the front door he swiftly shepherds the family into the waiting room, then beckons me to follow him and the sobbing child into his office. After closing the door behind us, Alex flashes me a hurried glance. "Elli, I'll need assistance. There's an extra white coat on the rack. Put it on. Then we must scrub fast."

After examining the sobbing little boy, Alex swiftly sets out the instruments and explains the name and function of each to me while keeping the little patient distracted with stories.

"Frankie, we have new goldfish in the tank. Can you see them? There are tiny baby ones and big ones with funny tails. Can you see the ones with the funny tails? Do you like goldfish, Frankie? Miss Friedman, are you ready? Please hand me each instrument as I ask for it. Okay?"

Frankie's sobs turn into chuckles as Dr. Hirschfield makes funny fish noises and carries on a dialogue between the mother fish and its baby. I assist Alex in holding the child down gently but firmly, shaving a patch around the wound, handing him the instruments for suturing the nasty cut, and bandaging the wound. When it is over, Alex pulls a red lollipop out of a drawer and hands it to the child. "This is for you, Frankie, for being so brave. Miss Friedman, would you like one too? You too deserve a lollipop!"

The Conegliaros are relieved to see their son emerge from the doctor's office with his head patched up, sucking on a lollipop.

"Doc, you are the greatest," the father shakes Alex's hand vigorously.

"Gracie. Gracie mucho," the mother whispers, and draping a protective arm about Frankie's shoulders, leads her family home in a glow of gratitude.

Alex and I look at our watches simultaneously. It's too late for the theater.

"I'm so sorry, sweetheart. I'll make it up to you."

"Never mind, Alex—we'll go another time. And besides, it was fun assisting you."

"You were great! A nurse couldn't have done a better job."

I am in heaven. "Really?"

"Would you be interested in doing this every Sunday? I was about to hire a nurse for Sunday mornings, from ten to twelve. You'd be paid as a trained nurse, fifteen dollars per session."

I am thrilled with Alex's offer, with the opportunity to assist him, to learn nursing skills, and to earn extra money. And above all I'm flattered that he considers me old enough—capable enough —for the job.

Sunday mornings become the happiest times of my life. It is a joy to work with Alex. My head is reeling with excitement from observing his great skill, his expert movements, his cool competence. My heart is full of admiration for his warm, easy manner with patients, for his wonderful sense of humor.

But the true adventure begins after work, when we repair to the living room. Alex shows me his latest painting, plays some of his musical compositions, and then encourages me to read selections from my poems. He lavishes undue praise on my talent, and I feel like Cinderella enclosed together with her Prince Charming in a bubble of bliss.

"Don't you think I should go to night school, to improve my English?" I ask Alex. "Don't you think it would improve my ability to express myself better?"

"I know of good courses given to new immigrants at Erasmus Hall High School. I believe you can still enroll for the summer. I will contact the school tomorrow, and call you when you get home from work," Alex promises.

Alex is good on his promise, and I'm thrilled to learn that enrollment is still open. Erasmus Hall High is on Flatbush and Church Avenues, not far from where we live. The next day I get off the subway on Flatbush Avenue on my way home, and make my way to the formidable building to register for the evening class.

My classes start at six thirty in the evening, and they end at ten. The bus ride home is only about twenty minutes, but there is a snag. With experience I learn that the Ocean Avenue bus reaches the corner of Church Avenue at ten fifteen, and if no one is waiting at the corner the driver does not even slow down but speeds past the bus stop. If I miss this bus there is a wait, sometimes as long as half an hour. To make sure I reach the corner before the bus approaches, I routinely run at a gallop nonstop from my classroom to the bus stop.

Tonight, a rather humid night, I find running a bit difficult yet reach the corner of Ocean and Church Avenue with a minute to spare. The minute passes and the bus is nowhere to be found, and on the dark, deserted the corner there are no other passengers waiting. Ten minutes pass, and the bus is not evident in the distance. What if I missed the last bus tonight? How will I get home? There are no taxis cruising down the avenue tonight . . . even if I had money for a taxi.

Suddenly a white Ford sedan pulls over to the curb. The driver rolls down the window. "Do you want a lift, miss?" he calls.

"Oh, thank you," I cry gratefully, and slide onto the passenger's seat. "How kind of you. I have been waiting for the bus for twenty minutes. . . . Do you drive down Ocean Avenue?"

"Yes, I do. Where do you live?"

"I live on Ocean, between O and P. Do you go that far?"

"Much beyond, all the way to Brighton Beach."

"Do you mind letting me off near Avenue O?"

"Will be happy to. No problem. Are you new in this country?"

"What makes you think so? My foreign accent?"

I notice that before answering my question the driver makes a right turn on Newkirk Avenue, then a left into a dark alley.

"Where are you going? This is not Ocean Avenue!"

"No, it is not."

"But you said you were driving down Ocean Avenue. I live on Ocean Avenue, and if you're not going there, I'd rather get out here."

The car comes to a stop. The driver reaches over to the passenger's door and locks it.

"No, you're not getting out here, miss. The door is locked."

Panic pounds on my temples.

"But . . . why?"

"Look here, miss. Because you are young and a new-comer in this country, I want to explain something to you. Never get into a stranger's car, especially late at night on a dark deserted street. New York is a dangerous city. . . . It's a very dangerous thing to do. I pulled into this side street deliberately to scare you. A man who picks up a young girl on a dark street corner has other intentions than to drop her off in front of her house a few blocks down. Do you understand?"

"I . . . I didn't know. Where I come from . . . Czechoslovakia . . . in Czechoslovakia we hitch rides on the highway all the time. There's no danger in it. It's done all the time. . . ."

"I figured. But here you must not do it. Never. Any girl who gets into a stranger's car the way you got into my car tonight is risking her life. That's why I wanted to teach you a lesson."

"Thank you," I whisper, my voice still strangled by panic. "But please will you get back to Ocean Avenue now?"

"Of course. The lesson is over. I hope you'll remember it always."

"I will. I am very grateful. . . ."

The car speeds on Ocean Avenue now and I let out an audible sigh of relief.

"Sorry, miss. Sorry to have frightened you. But it had to be done. What you did back there was wrong." The stranger's voice is suddenly heavy with fatigue. "A bit reckless."

The car comes to a standstill before our building. I open the passenger's door swiftly, calling one more thank you from the sidewalk, and the white Ford speeds off.

As I make my way to the entrance of the house and climb the front stairs, an involuntary shiver runs through my body.

"Elli, I think I found a solution for you—
for your ambition of teaching!" Bubi says one day, and his
face is alight with his discovery. "There are Jewish day
schools where Hebrew is taught in the morning, and the
regular curriculum in the afternoon, just like in a public
school," Bubi explains. "In the public school curriculum
a teacher is expected to have a college degree, but maybe
a Jewish Day School would accept your diploma from
the Beth Jacob Seminary in Bratislava, to teach Hebrew."

"Really? Where? Who should I contact? How can I
find out if I am qualified?"

"You can easily find out. There's a Jewish teachers'
association called the Jewish Education Committee. Why
don't you call them? They'll tell you about available positions. As a matter of fact, without the committee's sponsorship I don't believe you can get a teaching job. Phone
them as soon as you can."

Bubi teaches me how to use the telephone book, and
I manage to locate the number of the Jewish Education
Committee. On Monday I can barely wait for my lunch

hour, when I plan to make the phone call and take my first step toward my teaching career!

My hands tremble slightly as I hold the telephone receiver and listen to a voice at the other end asking, "Are you a member? You must apply for membership in person in order to receive services from the Committee."

Luckily there is an opening for an application interview during my lunch hour the next day. Before the interview I am given application forms to fill out, and on the basis of these the education officer informs me that I am not qualified for membership without a diploma from an accredited teachers' college or a B.A. degree with a major in education.

My arguments are in vain.

"Sorry, miss," the interviewer declares. "Your diploma from an eight-month crash course somewhere in Czechoslovakia is not acceptable here."

My explanations about lost educational opportunities because of the war, because of years spent in concentration and DP camps, and then in flight, make no impression. Neither do my letters of recommendation from the Beth Jacob schools in Bratislava and Vienna, from the public school in Camp Feldafing, the Hebrew Gymnasium, and the ORT School in Munich, and scores of letters from pupils and their parents attesting to my teaching skills. My application for membership in the Jewish Education Committee is rejected.

I decide to swallow my pride and appeal on humanitarian grounds. I plead hardship as a new immigrant for whom the Jewish Education Committee membership card would be tantamount to a lifeline.

The gentleman claims to be sympathetic to my dilemma but remains unmoved by my pleas. "Please bring us a valid teacher's diploma and we will be happy to issue you a membership card."

At the door I turn back sharply. "Okay," I shout in a flare of temper at the gray-haired official. "Deny me membership. It is your privilege. But I promise you, the day will come when you'll regret your decision! The day will come when you will offer me membership and I will refuse it!"

I walk out the door with measured footsteps, my legs trembling but my head held high.

Bubi is astonished at the J.E.C.'s decision. I think better of telling him about my outburst. *Impetuous as ever,* he would say. *Are you sure you're mature enough to become a teacher?* he would ask.

"Why don't you look in the Business section of the telephone book? Under the letter *Y* for *Yeshiva* you'll find the listing of the Hebrew day schools. They are open on Sundays. You can call them and see if they have any openings," Bubi advises, adding, "You have nothing to lose by trying."

After first telephoning every yeshiva listed in the Brooklyn, then in the Manhattan and Queens telephone books, I discover that no one will hire a teacher without a Hebrew teacher's diploma from an American institute or a membership card from the J.E.C. No yeshiva is willing to grant me an interview without one or the other.

Except one. At a school listed as Yeshiva of Central Queens the secretary refers me to a Mr. Gordon, who asks me to come and see him this afternoon. I am thrilled—I can't believe my luck. It is a brilliant Sunday afternoon, and I feel as if I sprouted wings—the hour-and-a-half subway ride from Brooklyn via Manhattan to Queens seems like I'm flying in a dream.

Mr. Gordon, a very tall gentleman with a gray mustache, introduces himself as the president of the school board and asks me to take a seat.

"As a rule, the principal does the hiring of teachers," Mr. Gordon begins. "But he is in Israel, and will be away all summer. I happened to be here today when you called. And I happen to know the school is looking for a first-grade Hebrew teacher. That's why I invited you to come down here this afternoon. I hope you don't mind," he adds with an apologetic smile. "Do you have experience teaching first grade?"

I respond by summarizing the history of my teaching career, and Mr. Gordon listens with fascination. "I am not an educator, nor a school administrator," Mr. Gordon apologizes once again. "I don't know Hebrew, and I don't know anything about teaching. I'm a businessman. I can only judge by personality. I believe you have the personality that a teacher should have. As a businessman I believe that with you we are getting a good deal. I am taking the liberty of offering you the position." Rising to his feet, Mr. Gordon extends his hand. "Miss Friedman, I hope you'll consider my offer. Will you let me know as soon as you can?"

I also rise, and put my hand into Mr. Gordon's large palm.

"Is now soon enough, Mr. Gordon?"

A wide smile brightens the agreeable face. "Soon enough, Miss Friedman. Welcome to the school. I hope you'll be happy here. I know the children will be lucky to have you," Mr. Gordon says warmly. "You'll receive written confirmation of the appointment by mail. As to the pay scale, it's standard. The contract will be drawn up with the principal when he returns."

I don't ask what *standard* means. All I know is: I have the job! The thrill vibrates through me as I skip along Jamaica Avenue toward the elevated train. I am a teacher again!

Isn't life magnificent? To be a teacher in America . . . a dream come true . . . without a teacher's diploma . . . without the precious J.E.C. membership card! And without even a high school diploma! But that's a deep, dark secret known only to a select few!

A week later when I receive the written confirmation, I give notice to Mr. Epstein. Sally and Evelyn, and even Miss Sokol, are sad to see me go. Leaving is more painful than I thought it would be.

Bubi, Mommy, Uncle Martin, and Aunt Celia share my happiness, and they are proud of my having landed a teaching job in America. But Uncle Martin has reservations about the school's location.

"Couldn't you have secured a job in Brooklyn?" he asks with concern. "It's madness to travel all that distance every day."

The distance does not worry me at all. I am drunk with happiness, and can't wait to share it with Alex.

Next Sunday I wait until after the hour of magic

when Alex and I share our creative endeavors. As Alex sits down to his grand piano and begins to play, the room fills with the heavenly sounds and my heart brims with a cavalcade of emotions. I must control the tremor that reverberates across my whole being, brings tears to my eyes. Alex must not see . . . must not notice. I would not be able to explain such an intense reaction to his music on my part. I myself don't understand it. Why do I feel piercing pain at my happiest moments? This commingling of pleasure and pain . . . why?

Thank God Alex does not look up or turn around when he completes a piece but goes on to the next, giving me ample time to compose myself. When he is through he rises and takes a playful bow toward me, his entire audience.

"Wie gefellt es Ihnen gnadige Fraulein?" (How do you like it, gracious young lady?) he asks with mock formality in German, and the lighthearted, comical gesture dispels my turbulent mood like magic.

"Wunderbar!" I exclaim, and we both laugh.

"Your poetry is next!" Alex sings out, and we sit next to each other on the couch, and I timidly hold two sheets of paper.

"I brought two poems," I say softly. "The others I wrote this week. . . . I don't know about them. I don't know if they're good enough. . . ."

"Let's hear these two now. Next week I hope you'll bring the others too."

I read my poems, one by one, first "The Beggar in Munich" and then "A Pile of Shoes," and Alex listens, his eyebrows drawn together with concentration, his eyes two shimmering indigo pools.

"Angel, what talent . . ." Alex murmurs. "These poems break the heart. Their deep sadness breaks my heart. You're but a child, so young . . . so full of effervescence, and yet . . . this heartbreaking sadness . . ." Alex reaches out and his large, warm hand encloses mine. "Angel, I want to make it up to you. I want to make this sadness disappear."

"Thank you, Alex. You already have."

"I want to make you happy, Elli. If you'll only let me."

Alex now takes both my hands into his and faces me with an intent look in his eyes, a secretive smile playing on his lips.

"This was to be a surprise, but I can't keep it a secret any longer," he says, and gives a happy sigh. "You know I have had plans for you . . . wonderful plans. You know, angel, I believe you'd make a superb laboratory technician. You have a scientific mind and deft hands—the makings of a first-class lab technician. Lab technicians are paid quite well. You can go far. And now, the surprise!"

My heart is pounding. I want to avert my face but can't: Alex's eyes are dancing with excitement—powerful magnets.

"I have enrolled you for a six-month course at the Mandel School for Medical Training!"

There is a momentary silence that seems to last forever. Alex is searching my eyes, my face, for my reaction, and I'm lost for words. Finally I burst out, deeply moved and desperate. "Oh, Alex . . . what can I say? Thank you for your generosity, for your concern. For your thoughtfulness. But . . . I want to be a teacher. That's what I've *always* wanted."

Alex does not seem to hear.

"As a lab technician you'd share my field," he continues, and his eyes reflect unclouded enthusiasm. "Later you'd specialize in hematology, and we will work together."

Alex is involved in leukemia research. He is passionate about this work, about his commitment to discover the cause of this dread disease. "You know what my secret dream is?" he asks, and his eyes scan my face with that look of bliss Aunt Celia ridiculed once and I have since come to love. "That you and I, working together as man and wife, will find a cure for cancer!

An icy cold hand tightens a grip on my throat.

In a flash Alex reads the panic in my face, and a deep furrow appears between his eyebrows. His eyes, now darker than I have ever seen, lock onto mine as he slowly intones with a voice as heavy as lead, "I know your answer, angel. You don't have to say it. You don't want to share my dream."

The sharp sting in Alex's words—his tone—is excruciating.

"Alex," I plead, and my voice drowns in tears. "You know I want to be a teacher. I was waiting to tell you. . . . I've gotten a job . . . was going to tell you today. I was saving it as a surprise."

Alex's face mirrors infinite sorrow. His voice drops to a hoarse murmur. "I'm losing you. You're arriving too fast in this country. Becoming too accomplished, too independent. You don't need me anymore. As long as you were new and helpless, I had hopes."

Alex's sad, brutal honesty cuts into raw flesh.

"Alex, isn't a relationship between equals preferable? My arriving—shouldn't it enhance our friendship?"

Alex's head hangs low.

"I have imagined . . . I have dreamed that you were Galatea to my Pygmalion. I fell in love with a young, ailing, frail, artless refugee, and dreamed of nurturing her to health and molding her in an image of my own making— a sophisticated woman of the world. I was wrong about you. You are not artless or frail. You are a strong woman; intelligent and capable, mature beyond your years. In a short time you have gone far. I'm losing you."

The air is charged with my sense of futility in the face of Alex's dejection. There is nothing I can do to alleviate his pain . . . my pain. Dr. Alexander Hirschfield—the fine doctor, energetic, brilliant, a man of irrepressible gusto and remarkable competence, a multitalented artist, grieving for the loss of his dream—is beyond consolation.

And I? Alex, I love you . . . need you. I need your strength, your friendship . . . your love. I need your embrace. I need you, Alex, now as much as ever.

And yet, all at once I realize with chilling certainty that I cannot have you. I can no longer welcome your love . . . not on your terms. Your love for me is wrapped up in your dream, and I am afraid I'm not ready to embrace such love. I'm not ready to be a slave to your dream. I must be free to pursue *my* dream. I must be free to grow . . . to find my own way in America.

Oh, God help me. Am I capable of paying this horrific price, of giving up all that Alex means to me? Am I capable of ending the fairy tale . . . bursting my bubble of bliss?

Chapter Fifteen

WHAT'S THAT NUMBER ON YOUR ARM?

As autumn arrives, Ocean Avenue is blanketed by brilliant yellow, orange, and burgundy leaves. The oppressive heat and harsh radiance of the long summer days are now replaced by the exhilarating chill of the early dusk, by lonely, lingering nightfall slipping into the night. There is a gentle, sad mystery in the air, a subtle premonition . . . a nameless promise that fills my heart with longing.

I long for Alex. The poignant beauty of autumn deepens the void that was Alex . . . the beauty that Alex was to my life.

But autumn also means the beginning of the school year—the beginning of my teaching career in America. Teaching first grade is as thrilling as I had hoped, and bit by bit the void begins to fill.

Although I expected American children to be different, the little six-year-old boys and girls are in many ways just like the children I taught in the transit camp in Vienna and in the refugee camp in Feldafing, Germany, just as eager to learn and just as ready to be loved.

LIVIA BITTON-JACKSON

I have a need to dispense both—learning and love.
Sometimes I wonder, are the two not one and the same?
I believe for me they are. For me sharing knowledge is
sharing love. The Talmud teaches: "Words that come from
the heart, enter the heart." These small American boys
and girls in my class seem to respond to my "words from
the heart" with the same enthusiasm as did my little
charges in the refugee camps.

The difference between teaching in Europe and
teaching in America lies in the method of discipline. Very
quickly I learn that American children are not accustomed to sitting perfectly still in the classroom. Neither
are they accustomed to a slap on the wrist, a most natural element of the European classroom.

My fellow teachers are aghast when during recess I
tell them that I slapped little Phillip on the wrist for fidg-
eting and talking in class.

"What is *cops*?" I ask. "He threatened to call the cops."

Uproarious laughter greets my words, then one
teacher explains, "*Cops* is another word for police. But
this is serious. You committed a grievous error."

"What error?" I ask, taken aback.

"Didn't you know that in America no manner of
physical punishment is allowed?"

I'm truly shocked at this news. "No manner of physical punishment? But . . . how can you teach without an
occasional slap?"

"You'll learn," my colleagues advise, and I take their
warning to heart.

My task is to teach my little pupils elementary

Hebrew—to read and write Hebrew characters, and to master a basic Hebrew vocabulary. Teaching a new language to such young children is a wonderful challenge. My pupils and I together participate in the daily adventure of learning new words and new concepts; together we experience the great fun of beginning to speak a new language.

Besides fun, there's something else.

As I stand before the classroom of eager childish faces, I am overcome by a sense of the enormity of my survival—a validation. Ever since that fateful day when Dr. Joseph Mengele, the "Angel of Death" in Auschwitz, pulled me out of the line leading to the gas chambers, I've been plagued by agonizing guilt: Why me? Why me? Why was I spared from among my friends? Why was I granted life while they all died?

This classroom of children helps assuage my guilt. My commitment to dispense learning and love is my raison d'être—my justification for being alive.

The Hebrew classes end at noon. When the bell rings we file out of the classroom, and as we line up in the corridor and march to the lunchroom, and even during lunch, we continue our game of speaking Hebrew. After lunch I accompany my pupils back to the classroom for their afternoon session, and we say good-bye to each other. They remain in class for the regular public school curriculum in English, taught by a new shift of educators, and I join the two other Hebrew first-grade teachers on the subway ride home.

Mrs. Lichtenstein and Miss Brandwein also live in

Brooklyn, and the three of us travel together part of the way, sharing snippets of our lives, getting to know each other during the hour's journey every afternoon.

During the third week I am summoned to the principal's office. Oh, my God, the principal must have found out about the slap on Phillip's wrist!

My legs tremble as I enter the office.

"Miss Friedman," the principal gets to the point without preliminaries. "I must admit, when I returned from Israel and discovered that Mr. Gordon had hired you, I was upset," he says with a frown. "No certificates, no formal education? How could he take such action? Yet there was nothing we could do. Mr. Gordon had given his word, in the name of the school, in writing. We consulted a lawyer, and he confirmed what we already knew: A written commitment is like a contract and could not be broken. But the lawyer advised us to watch you closely. He advised that at the first mistake, we had the right to dismiss you." I take a deep breath. . . . Here it comes. . . . This is the end. "These past three weeks were your trial period, and I am letting you know that you've made it. After observing you teaching, relating to the children, I am compelled to agree with Mr. Gordon. He believed you were a born teacher. I just can't understand how he knew."

I walk out of the principal's office on cloud nine. I can't believe it. The principal, instead of dismissing me because of the slap, praised me for my teaching! Thank you, my God, thank you. I promise I'll be the best teacher I can ever be!

My heady ride on cloud nine lasts less than a week. At

the first monthly staff meeting the principal turns to me with a frown. "Miss Friedman, see me in my office right after the meeting." And I suddenly find myself down on earth.

Oh, no, the news of the slap has finally caught up with me.

The principal launches into the subject as soon as I enter the office. "Miss Friedman, we've received serious complaints about you."

"Complaints? What complaints?"

"Parents called me with indignation, I might say with alarm, that you're frightening the children with atrocity stories. You're spreading horror stories in the school. . . ."

"Horror stories? Rabbi, what are you talking about?"

"The children reported that you told the class you were in a concentration camp."

"Concentration camp? I have never . . ." All at once I remember. "Ah yes. A little boy in class, I think it was Baruch Sturm, noticed the number on my arm and asked what it was. I replied that it was done in the concentration camp, where we had numbers instead of names. That's all I said. I didn't elaborate. I had been warned not to talk about the camps, was told people in America didn't want to hear . . . to know about what happened. And I certainly wouldn't talk to first-graders about the horrors . . . But since the pupil posed a question, I had no choice but to provide a truthful answer—as direct and as simple an answer as I could."

"You shouldn't have given that answer," the Rabbi says disapprovingly.

"What other answer could I have given?"

"You should have answered it was your telephone number."

"What! My telephone number, tattooed on my arm?"

The principal's shiny black desk assumes an other-worldly dimension as I stand before it, grappling with the principal's words. "Rabbi, do you want me to tell a lie to my pupils?" It takes great effort to control the trembling in my voice. "Do you want my answer to imply that they have a madwoman for a teacher who tattoos her telephone number on her arm? And what happens if I move and change telephone numbers? What is your suggestion, Rabbi?" I can no longer contain my voice, and it rises to a fever pitch. "What is your suggestion, Rabbi?"

Despite my anguish I am aware that the questions I have hurled at the principal only camouflage the storm in my soul. They do not even touch on the banality of his remark . . . the blatant triteness that in one flippant swoop trivialized the tragedy of the Holocaust of our people—both his and mine.

The principal does not lose his cool. In an even voice he says, "No matter what, my reply would have been preferable to the one you gave."

As I stand there a chasm opens between us, with the rabbi sitting solidly on the far side of the abyss and me standing at the edge of the precipice that is getting wider and wider threatening to engulf my world.

Unaware of the offensive nature of his remark and of the abyss it has opened between us, the rabbi, with the frown on his face somewhat faded, delivers his final warning: "I hope you'll remember what I've told you, Miss Friedman."

I will remember. I will remember as long as I live. . . .

In my pain and bitterness I wonder, do all Americans, Jews and Gentiles who were untouched by our tragedy and don't even want to hear about it, feel like him? Do they also prefer to believe that the number tattooed on my arm in Auschwitz is nothing but a harmless New York telephone number? Do they also prefer to place me, and all of us with numbers tattooed on our arms, beyond the pale of their world?

Chapter Sixteen

MOTHER HAS A JOB

Mother lands a job as a finisher in a workshop called Ripley's on the Upper West Side of Manhattan, manufacturing men's suits and coats.

"What's a *finisher*?" I ask. "What a funny word."

"It's not funny for us newcomers," Aunt Celia remarks, laughing. "Hey, just because you're a teacher—a professional—but the rest of us, we all are finishers. . . . Your uncle, I, and all our friends—and now your mother. A finisher works on the assembly line, adding a part to the piece under production. As you know, I stitch lining into ties; your uncle, into hats."

"I put lining into men's suit jackets," Mother adds. "Then pass it on the assembly line to the next worker, who puts on buttons . . . whatever."

I learn another new word—*piece worker*. Mother is a piece worker at Ripley's. Piece workers are paid per piece—lining stitched, sleeves set, or buttons sewn—and so their earnings depend on the number of pieces they manage to complete by the end of the workday. Their earnings depend on speed.

"Speed is almighty God in the workshop," Mother observes after a few days at the factory. "There is a sort of competition going on for the number of pieces done at the end of the day, not just for money. It's a contest of skill, stamina, cleverness, even youth. At the end of the workday when the foreman announces the number of pieces done by each worker, you can hear a pin drop." Mother says in amazement.

"They kill themselves to win," she goes on, shaking her head. "Win at all cost. Some don't even take lunch breaks. And what do they win at the end of the day? A moment of glory, a few extra cents, and a ferocious pain in the lower back."

At the beginning there is grumbling on the line as Mother's slower pace affects the flow of goods farther along the line, but then the foreman notices the superior quality of Mother's sewing—how much finer her stitches are— and he works out an accommodation, allowing her pieces to be set aside for the buttonhole makers, whose work is done at a less hectic tempo.

In the morning Mother and I travel together to work. Rising at the crack of dawn, I love the adventure of tiptoeing around in the dark living room where we sleep, whispering to each other so as not to wake Aunt Celia and Uncle Martin in the bedroom, then leaving the house soundlessly and making our way to the subway station in semidarkness. By the time we reach Kings Highway, the rising day splatters an eerie light on the deserted avenue ordinarily swarming with human traffic, and on the shuttered storefronts and fruit stands now cozily wrapped in layers of canvas. There is a sense of mystery—a sense of power—in being here before the rest of the world awakens . . . as if witnessing the beginning of time.

We love traveling together on the subway, Mother and I. It's fun to observe our fellow subway riders, exchange jokes and asides in Hungarian, play guessing games as to their identities, their ages, and their jobs and make bets as to where they'd be getting off.

In a couple of weeks Mother becomes familiar with the train route, and she no longer allows me to accompany her.

"But I'll miss the fun of traveling together in the morning," I protest.

"So will I. But it comes at a sacrifice. In order to accompany me you must rise an hour earlier, losing an hour's sleep. You need that extra hour of sleep." Mother is firm, and I have no choice but to comply and regretfully give up on our morning fun.

"I hope you'll have time to teach me English. Now that I have a job and travel alone on the subway, I'll need to improve my vocabulary. I don't want to depend on you every time I need to make a phone call in English, or want to take public transport."

"Okay, madam," I agree in a happy, jocular tone. "How about today? Let's have our first lesson this evening!"

Every evening I grill Mother in vocabulary and grammar, and indeed in a couple of weeks she learns enough English to do marketing on her own and travel freely by subway.

The subway train becomes an integral part of our lives. I no longer suffer panic attacks after the doors close, converting the car into a hermetically sealed container. On the contrary, the total detachment and alienation of the passengers from one another, which at first shocked and saddened me, I now perceive as an asset. I enjoy the anonymity it provides. In the crowded subway car I am free to do as I please without interruptions. I even relish the rush hour and its blessing of absolute privacy!

The only requirement for optimum subway bliss is to secure a seat. After a short research I discover that the 6:20 A.M. train—a perfect timing for my eight o'clock class—has available seats in the last car. Once I settle in my seat, the subway car becomes my private study. Propped on my knee, my briefcase becomes my desk on which to write letters, grade my little pupils' homework, and compose poetry once again.

But once an incident in the subway reopens unhealed wounds. One afternoon on my homebound ride, a husky, blond Amazon in a nurse's white shoes and stockings leans confidentially close to me and, thrusting her chin in the direction of a young woman standing nearby, says in an undertone, "These Jewish women. They are so brazen. They have no manners, no taste."

While I listen, incredulous, she goes on, "Do you see her? She is pregnant and look how she's flaunting her pregnancy."

"What are you talking about?" I ask, and, convinced that she was crazy, I draw slightly aside.

"When I was pregnant I always wore a coat, a big

loose coat to cover my body. Even in the summer I wouldn't go out without a coat. We were brought up with good taste. But these Jewish women . . . they are vulgar, brazen hussies. . . . Heh!" As she speaks she shoots a gaze of utter disgust at the young woman who doesn't even look pregnant to me. In my shock and disbelief I respond with the first of many questions that rush to my mind.

"How do you know she's Jewish?"

"I can tell a Jew anywhere!"

"Can you? Would you take me for a Jew?"

"You? Oh, no. Certainly not! You must be German."

I pull up my sleeve. "Do you see this?"

She looks at the number tattooed on my arm. "What is this?"

The blood rushes to my face. I'm shaking. I lose my cool. "This number was put on my arm in Auschwitz by people like you!" I scream. My voice must have shattered the interminable din because at once a dead hush descends on the subway car and all eyes turn in our direction.

The woman's face is livid. "I'm not German. Only my husband is a German," she shouts. "My parents came over from Germany many years ago and I was born here. I'm an American!"

"You don't have to be German to be anti-Semitic," I shout back. "I don't care whether you're German or not, but you're an anti-Semite. People like you put six million Jews to death!"

At this point the train pulls into the station, the doors

open, and the husky blond woman runs out of the car. The subway audience bursts into applause, and I burst out crying.

I cry with embarrassment, with the mortification for having made a spectacle of myself, for having lost control—for exposing my vulnerabilities.

And yet the applause in the subway car is my vindication. It has answered a question I was afraid to ask. Their hearty applause told me that all these subway riders disagreed with the blond Amazon's senseless prejudice . . . that they were not on the side of the killers. It provided me with the answer. Most Americans were not anti-Semitic.

I pray for this to be true. For me to be happy in my new world I must believe it to be true.

Chapter Seventeen

A HOLIDAY IN THE CATSKILLS

My subway episode comes as a shock to the family. Especially Uncle Martin, the idealist, is incredulous. "I wouldn't have believed such views are possible in America," he says and his voice betrays deep disappointment.

The ringing of the telephone interrupts the discussion, and when he hangs up the phone, Uncle Martin's eyes sparkle with excitement. The anti-Semitic encounter seems to be forgotten.

"You have just been invited for a holiday in the Catskills," he announces. "For the entire Sukkoth holiday: eight days."

"In the Catskills?" I ask, astonished. "In the Catskill Mountains? Who has invited us? And why?"

"It's a 'welcome to America' gesture. They heard about your arrival."

"Who's 'they'?"

"You know my cousins, the Wallersteins? Well, the family owns resort hotels in the Catskill Mountains. One is the Mountain View Hotel and the other, the Pine Forest. We are invited to the Pine Forest. It's run by my cousin Nina, her son, and daughter-in-law. It was Nina's daughter-in-law, Emily, who has just called."

The Catskill Mountains have occupied a special place in my imagination ever since I read about their magic spell in an English reader I found while foraging for food in the rubble of an American army base. The book became my Bible for learning English. I memorized every word of every story even before I knew the meaning of the words or how to pronounce them. The first story was the legend of Rip Van Winkle, the Dutch colonist who went hunting in the Catskill Mountains of New York, only to meet a group of strange little men. Dazed from their liquor, Rip Van Winkle lay down to take a nap but fell asleep for twenty years. When he awoke and returned to his village, he was astonished to find everything changed, as if by magic.

This strange tale became one with the Catskill Mountains in my mind. I have often wondered what it would be like to sleep high in the mountains and to drop out of life for twenty years. How would that feel? How would I cope with it?

Three years ago Mother and I spent a happy summer in the scenic Carpathian mountain range in a camp for orphaned children where I worked as assistant counselor. In my free time the two of us went hiking in the hills and boating on the mountain lake, and I remembered the tale of the Catskill Mountains. Since then mountain hiking has remained an impossible dream. Until now.

"Mommy . . . Bubi, isn't it great? We'll be in the mountains for Sukkoth!"

"I'm so sorry, Elli. But the invitation does not include your mother. And I'm sorry to say, not your brother either. Only you," Uncle Martin says.

"Why not them? I can't leave them behind. How can I leave the two of them behind while I'm cavorting in the Catskills? Uncle, I'm afraid I cannot . . . I'll have to decline the invitation."

"Don't be a fool. Such invitations don't come a dime a dozen. Who knows when you will have another chance to spend a holiday at such a luxurious resort? And the two of them, your mother and your brother, they'll be happy spending the holiday together. And they'll be happy for you. Just don't be rash. Think before you decline."

The vote is unanimous. Both Mother and Bubi insist that I go with my aunt and uncle to the Pine Forest Hotel for the Sukkoth holiday.

"What will you wear?" Mother, as always, instantaneously confronts practicalities. "Other than the pale blue outfit and red coolie coat Lilly and Abish bought you, you have no dressy clothes. You need at least one more outfit to wear in an elegant place like that. You can't show up looking like a poor refugee."

Uncle Martin brings home a bolt of cloth, a remnant, from the factory, a deep forest green fabric. "How do you like it?" he asks Mother. "An ideal color for Elli. I believe blondes should always wear green. Especially blondes with green eyes."

"It's perfect!" Mother exclaims, measuring the cloth. "Enough for a skirt and a bolero. I'll get a lighter green remnant, perhaps silk, for a matching blouse."

I watch helplessly as Mother works like a fiend in her free time, cuts and measures and sews, the old, battered Singer machine we borrowed whirring late into the night to have the outfit ready in time for my vacation in the Catskills. I have to stand still while Mother tries the blouse on me, then the skirt, while she pins up the hem and adjusts the sleeves, and marks the spots for the buttons. I hate to stand still. I don't need a new dress, I don't need all this fuss—all I want is to roam the forest where Rip Van Winkle met Henry Hudson's funny little men and then slept for twenty years.

The day of our trip arrives, and my new outfit, a flared skirt and a bolero—a sleeveless short jacket, the "latest fashion rage"—and a matching green silk blouse with large white polka dots and puffed sleeves, is ready. One of my colleagues at Yeshiva of Central Queens lends me a pair of shorts and a matching top, and my gear for an adventure in the mountains is complete.

At Pennsylvania Station, Celia, Martin, and I board a Greyhound bus bound for South Fallsburg in New York State, the nearest town to the hotel. From there the Pine Forest Hotel is a short taxi ride.

The bus travels north, then northwest through New York State in the lap of astonishing luxury of nature— deep green forests dotted with lakes and cascading waterfalls, the road rising higher and higher into the bewitching world of the Catskill Mountains.

From the moment of our arrival I'm intoxicated with the resort's grounds—the Olympic-size pool, the tennis courts, the elegant lobby, the lavish reception with glamorous women and men sporting deep tans! I feel as if I have been transported into paradise.

"Tennis?" He is a tall man with dark complexion and dark glasses.

"Me?" I take a deep breath. "I don't play. Sorry."

"Why not?" He cocks his head and his shiny brown curls fall to one side.

"I . . . I don't know how."

"Really? I can teach you."

"But I can't. . . . I . . . I don't have an outfit for tennis."

"What you have on is fine."

"For tennis? You must wear white . . . a white top and skirt, a tennis skirt . . ."

"Only on a proper tennis court. Here in the country you can wear whatever you want. Your shorts and top are fine. You want to play? You want to learn?" Now his head is cocked even farther to one side, and a coaxing smile plays on his face.

"Well, I must warn you, I really don't know how to play. I'm very clumsy. You'll be frustrated and bored before you'll succeed in teaching me."

"Thank you for the warning. I'll take note. The rest is up to me."

After the first half hour of uselessly hopping around missing the ball but not the net, I learn to anticipate the ball and return it more or less accurately. The next two hours are pure magic. I take great delight in striking the ball and watching it fly over the net, in meeting the oncoming shots, and striking again and again.

"Brava!" The handsome stranger yells. "Bravissima! You are good! How about a cool drink? I'm parched."

"*Parched* means *thirsty*?"

"Very thirsty. Are you new to English? By the way, my name is Roberto. Roberto Radames. And yours?"

"Elli. Elli Friedman."

"Are you a newcomer in the country?"

"What's today? September twenty-eighth? I've been here twenty-two weeks."

"That's all? And your English is not bad."

"I learned English before I came."

"And tennis two hours ago. You learn fast."

We sip orange juice from tall glasses through thin plastic straws, just like Sally and Evelyn did with the milk shake.

"Why sip through a straw?" I wonder. "It doesn't seem like an efficient method, too slow when you're thirsty."

Roberto gives a hearty chuckle. "You're right. But it's too late. We've finished our drinks."

At dinner I introduce Roberto to Aunt Celia and Uncle Martin, and the two exchange glances. Later when we are alone, both Celia and Martin bombard me with questions about the "tall, dark, handsome Latin type." Where is he from? What does he do? How old is he?

I find out that Roberto also is not American-born. He came from Portugal with his parents and older brother twelve years ago, when he was fourteen. He works as a dental technician, and lives with his parents on Manhattan's Upper West Side.

Roberto and I strike a deal—Hebrew for tennis. As Roberto admittedly does not have an extensive Jewish education and does not know any Hebrew but is eager to learn, on our walks I agree to teach him the basics of Hebrew and Judaism.

On the last day Nina's son, Miki, asks me to give "a short talk" about the Sukkoth holiday during the farewell dinner.

"Gladly," I reply. "It'll give me the opportunity to thank your parents for this fantastic vacation."

It is a beautiful event in the lavishly decorated sukkah. As I look about me at the opulent company seated around the richly laden tables, my self-confidence plummets like a dead bird. Miki is the master of ceremonies, and when it is my turn to speak, his extravagant introduction makes me wish the earth swallowed me. But when I rise to talk, the wholehearted applause of the guests inspires a bit of courage and I deliver my talk in English without a major mishap! At the conclusion of my little lecture I'm deeply moved by the generous reception from the management and the guests, especially when I see my uncle and aunt's faces beaming with pride.

After dinner I am swamped by the guests' questions and flattering comments, and "my cup runneth over." Isn't America wonderful? Such bighearted acceptance of my very first lecture in America . . . delivered in English!

I am eager to hear Roberto's comments, and I make a beeline in his direction. But Roberto does not comment. He seems distant. When it's time to leave he gives me a rather cool farewell, without a single reference to all the plans he proposed only yesterday for our dating in the city.

Why? What has gone wrong?

I turn to Miki for an explanation.

"Your lecture tonight did it," Miki replies. "American men are afraid of eggheads. . . . An egghead for a girl-friend?" He shudders. "Especially if she's a blonde. A blond bombshell turned egghead—what a fiasco! I pity the guy."

What's a bombshell? What's an egghead? What is Miki talking about?

Miki, my new tutor, explains the meaning of both. I still don't understand.

"Why can't a blonde be both a bombshell and an egghead?"

"It just doesn't happen. Doesn't work."

If you want boys—men—to like you, to be comfortable with you, you keep your mouth shut. Don't let them find out you are smart. Is this how it works in America?

Two days after our return to New York, Roberto telephones and asks to see me. We set a date for Sunday afternoon, and Roberto arrives with a bouquet of flowers. When at first he is tense, awkwardly searching for words, I try to ease his discomfort by dismissing the issue. I appreciate his courage. It takes guts to confront an unpleasant issue and to apologize, and I tell him so.

Although our date ends on a happy note, something has changed. Roberto's conduct confirms Miki's observations about bombshells and eggheads. I understand

Roberto mistook me for an empty-headed blonde. . . .
And now I no longer want to be his steady date.

Perhaps one day I will meet a guy for whom I will be
neither a bombshell nor an egghead—but just me.

I think of Alex. Alex loved me not for my blond looks
but for my capacity to learn, to absorb. For my talent. But
Alex wanted to remake me in his image.

I must call Sally and Evelyn. Ever since I left the
Jewish National Fund almost two months ago, we have
kept up contact via telephone. I must speak to them
about Roberto, to sound them out, to get their help in
figuring out all the confusion in my head.

Chapter Eighteen

A BLIND DATE

Tonight Sally's phone call comes as a fluky surprise.

"How did you know I needed to talk to you?" I cry into the mouthpiece. "For days now I intended calling you! Is Evelyn with you?"

"I'm here, Elli!" Evelyn pipes up on the other line. "Hi!"

When I tell them the Roberto saga, both girls advise me not to go steady.

"Not until you meet Mr. Right," Sally adds.

"I'm not going steady. But should I go out with him at all? After what happened?"

"What happened is not so horrendous," Evelyn says. "Give him a second chance."

"Just because he panicked after he heard your lecture . . . well, I wouldn't say that's earth-shattering. Get to know him a little better before you dump him," Sally advises.

"But do not agree to go out with him Saturday night if he phones after Thursday," Evelyn adds. "Even

Thursday is a bit late. But definitely not Thursday evening, or Friday."

"Suppose he was busy during the week and couldn't call."

"Tough luck," the two of them shout in unison into the telephone receiver.

"You say you're busy on Saturday night," Sally continues. "A girl should never be available for a date if the guy calls on Thursday evening, and forget about it if he calls on Friday."

Luckily Roberto calls early in the week, and we set a date for Saturday night. I enjoy his company, but the spark kindled on the tennis court is gone. He seems ordinary. And I am embarrassed to admit it, but I am troubled by some of his idiosyncrasies, his habit of using the phrase *frankly speaking* in every third or fourth sentence and the word *great* to describe almost anything he likes. "Get to know him before you dump him," Sally advised. I decide to follow Sally's advice.

On Sunday morning Roberto unexpectedly telephones, his voice halting, hesitant.

"Are you free this afternoon. . . . Can we meet?"

I am baffled. I must do preparations for my class at the yeshiva. Yet there is something urgent in Roberto's tone, so I accept the invitation.

"I can be free in the afternoon, Roberto, if you wish to meet."

The sky is overcast and rain hangs in the air when Roberto arrives. He asks that we go on a long drive, "somewhere . . . anywhere."

"Sunday afternoons I have the Monday-morning blues," he confesses. "I just had to see you."

We drive around the beachfront, then head for Prospect Park and drive around the lake in the center of the park. "Sunday afternoons it is hard to face the week...." he says in a thin voice. "By Monday afternoon it is easier. If only Mondays never happened . . . if we never had to face life," Roberto says in a whisper.

Roberto drives aimlessly, and I search my mind for amusing things to entertain him, to drive away the "Monday-morning blues"—whatever they are.

"Thank you for this great outing," Roberto says two hours later as he pulls alongside the curb near the entrance of our apartment building. "Frankly speaking, this is a first. I've never had such a lovely way to beat the blues."

"I am happy it worked," I say awkwardly, not knowing what to do next, what Roberto is going to do next.

Roberto sits still in the driver's seat, looking ahead, his eyes fixed on the windshield, on the raindrops as they dance mercilessly on the glass. Then he turns to me, and his face, his eyes, are brimming with sadness. "Elli, you're a great girl. Thank you again for the greatest Sunday afternoon of my life."

What's going on? Is he going to park? Is he going to walk me to my door? Or is this good-bye, right here in the car? We both wait in the no-man's-land of silence. I open the car door.

"I am happy you feel better, Roberto. I hope you feel able to face the week."

Roberto nods. I wave to him from the sidewalk, and he revs the engine.

Days and then weeks go by and Roberto doesn't call. Why? What happened?

Neither Sally nor Evelyn can figure it out.

Why am I tormented so by Roberto's behavior, by his not calling? I am not in love, was dating him only to "give it a chance," whatever "it" was. Then what troubles me so—the unknown? The unexplained? Being rejected? Was I actually rejected? Even that I don't know.

"You need a new date," Sally prescribes a cure. "You must meet someone nice, not a lunatic like that Roberto."

"Lillian's giving a party, it's going to be a chicken market. You may meet someone there."

"A chicken market? What's that?"

"A singles' party. Guys looking for girls. No pretenses. Everyone there is looking. Come with us; you'll meet someone."

"But I don't know Lillian. How can I show up at her party without an invitation?"

"You don't need an invitation to a chicken market. People hear about it through the grapevine. Besides, you know us. We are inviting you."

I tell my brother about the chicken market. He knows all about chicken markets but has never been to one. "I don't think it's for you," he muses. "It's too American." The he remembers: "Mr. Rosenfeld phoned while you were out. He wants to introduce you to his nephew. Asked that you call him back."

"Who is Mr. Rosenfeld?"

"He's Uncle Abish's friend, the banker. He met you at their house. He wants you to call him up, and he'll set up the meeting with the nephew. Just call him. What can you lose?"

Bubi hands me the notepaper with Mr. Rosenfeld's phone number, and I dial. Mr. Rosenfeld is not in his office, and I leave a message with his secretary. When Mr. Rosenfeld returns my call, he gets straight to the point. His nephew is a decent fellow, makes a good living, is looking for a wife, and Mr. Rosenfeld believes I am the right match.

"You two should meet on a blind date and take it from there," he says cheerfully, matter-of-factly.

"What's a blind date?"

"When a boy and girl go out on a date without having met before. American girls don't like to go on blind dates; it's below them. But you are a new immigrant. You shouldn't hesitate."

"Still, I'd like to know something about your nephew before I go out with him."

"What do you have to know? I told you everything there is to know. He's a decent fellow with a good income. His name is Neal. I'll give him your phone number, and he'll call you."

"Is he . . . what's his educational background?"

"You mean, is he a high school graduate? He is."

"How about college?"

"No college. He's a decent fellow—what more do you want?"

"Did he go to a yeshiva?"

"Even yeshiva you want? You know, girls like you shouldn't be so picky. You should be happy to get a decent fellow."

"Girls like me . . . what do you mean by that, Mr. Rosenfeld?"

"I saw the number on your arm. We all know what happened over there, in the camps. We heard how young girls like you survived by entertaining the German soldiers. Those who refused were killed. Only those who were willing to survive at any price made it. Girls like that should be grateful if a decent fellow in America is willing to marry them."

"Thank you, Mr. Rosenfeld," I say with a steady voice, and place the telephone receiver in its cradle. A minute later it rings again. It's Mr. Rosenfeld.

"What happened? You hung up? But I wasn't finished."

"Yes, you were, Mr. Rosenfeld," I say steadily like a robot, and like a robot once again place the receiver in its cradle.

"What's going on?" My brother asks, and when I tell him slowly, quietly, my voice hoarse with emotion, my brother's eyes fill with a flame I cannot identify. Is it pain? Sadness? Is it helpless rage?

On Saturday night I go to Lillian's chicken market.

The narrow corridor is lined, one side girls, the opposite side boys, engaged in noisy conversation punctuated with shrieks, laughter, and horseplay. It is incredibly crowded and I can see neither Sally nor Evelyn. I must get out. I am ready to flee but a long leg in gray trousers blocks my path.

"Are you leaving already? We haven't even met."

"Sorry. It's too noisy for me here. Too crowded. If you don't mind . . ." I point at the leg. "I'd like to pass."

He draws his leg out of my path, and I make my way, painstakingly, to the exit. The owner of the gray trouser leg follows me to the door. "May I walk with you? It's too noisy for me, too."

As I reach for the doorknob, his gaze falls on the number on my arm. I can see shock register in the brown eyes.

"I . . . I would prefer to walk alone. Forgive me. Good night."

"Good night."

Chapter Nineteen

ALEX IS BACK

Tonight I am unable to elude my nightmares, to employ my skill so finely honed throughout the years, to let them float away like a kite and slip beneath them into sleep. Tonight my nightmares have the upper hand. I flee desperately but the rabbi waves a number in the air. . . . I know that number well. It's not my phone number. Mr. Rosenfeld's nephew keeps dialing the number, and I'm haunted by the sound of incessant ringing as the bloodhounds pounce on the telephone and I shriek, "It's not my telephone number. . . . Can you hear?" But they pounce on me and maul my arm. The numbers bleed as the telephone rings on and on. . . .

I reach for the receiver. "Hello . . . hello."

Mother is awakened by my voice. "Who are you talking to? It's the middle of the night."

"Wrong number. Let's go back to sleep."

I toss and turn for the rest of the endless, interminable night.

I need someone to help me cope with the turmoil in my soul, with this hurt that gnaws at my insides. To whom can I turn? Not Mother. How can I burden her? And Bubi, I saw the pain in his eyes when I told him of Mr. Rosenfeld's insinuation. Aunt Celia or Uncle Martin . . . how can I inflict fresh agony on them? And besides, their reaction would only intensify mine. Sally and Evelyn, and even Judy and her friends, belong to another world . . . another planet.

Alex! He would understand. He would sense my pain. Oh, how I miss him! How I miss his caring, his fatherly concern, his wide, masculine shoulders . . . his strength!

I go about my Sunday-morning chores with the restlessness of a caged lion, helping Aunt Celia and Mother with housecleaning, laundry, ironing. When I dismiss Mother's repeated questions about what's bothering me, she chalks it up to "that time of the month" and begins to fuss.

"Why don't you have a glass of warm milk and crawl into bed? You'll feel better after a short nap. Leave the ironing to us. Here," Mommy hands me a glass, and pours milk into it from the pot on the stove. "Drink it, Elli."

Balancing the glass of milk on a small tray, I go to the bedroom and carefully close the door behind me. With trembling fingers I dial Alex's telephone number. What will he say? How will he say it? His tone—will it be icy or hoarse with resentment? Will he call me to task? Or just hang up as soon as he hears my voice?

"Hello?" My heart beats so loud I can barely hear my own voice. "Hello?"

"Hello? Who's this? Elli? Is it really you?" The familiar

voice, the same caressing, warm tone. My heart leaps to my throat.

"Yes, it's me, Alex. . . . How are you?"

"I can't believe you actually called me! How are *you*?" Time stands still. Nothing has changed. Oh, it's just like before. "Elli, are you there?"

"Yes, Alex, I'm here. I was just wondering . . . can we meet some time? Any time you are free."

"I am free . . . now. Do you want to meet today? This afternoon? I can come right over."

"Right now? Yes, I'm free right now. Alex . . . I'll wait for you downstairs."

A tremor passes through my body as I place the telephone receiver in its cradle. Whatever possessed me to do this, to invite Alex to come over? All I wanted was to hear his voice, to talk to him on the telephone. What changed my resolve? Was it his voice, the caring in his voice? And now what have I started?

"Where are you going?" Mother wants to know.

"Oh, just out. I won't be long."

"For a walk? It's much too cool outside. You haven't been feeling well all morning. Is it wise to go for a walk? At least take your warm overcoat."

I cannot lie to Mother. I would rather risk her annoyance at my behavior than lie. Mother, Bubi, Celia, and Martin leapt for joy when Alex and I broke up. They were concerned that I wouldn't be able to stand up to the challenge of Alex's barrage of phone calls. But when the phone calls died out and weeks passed without Alex and I seeing each other, everyone brightened as if a cloud passed from their horizon.

"I'm not walking. I'm going for a ride."

"A ride? With whom?"

"With Alex."

"Alex?" Mother's eyes are wide blue saucers.

"Don't worry, Mom. I won't be long."

As she sees me to the door, Mother's face is white alabaster and her lips are a tight line drawn with a thin pencil.

"Please, Mom, don't worry. I'll be back within the hour."

I skip down the stairs, two at a time. In front of the building Alex flings open the car door. His joy is open like the cloudless sky, and I bask in its glow.

"Angel, I missed you."

"I missed you, too, Alex."

"Let's go to our favorite place, okay?"

I nod silently, and Alex drives south on Ocean Avenue toward the beach, until he reaches the bay where fishing boats bob on the waves. At night the moon used to sway here among them. But it's still too early for the moon, the sky is overcast, and a dark mist rises among the boats.

"Are you in the mood for a milk shake?" Alex asks, laughing. Alex remembers my love of milk shakes.

"A wonderful idea." I play along. "A milk shake would be just perfect!"

The cafe on Seagirt Avenue is empty, and we take a seat in the corner that affords an unimpeded view of the wharf. The sweet, creamy liquid has an instant effect on my spirits.

"Now, angel, tell me, did you call because you missed me? Or was there something troubling you . . . something that you wanted to talk about? Please understand, I'm happy as long as you called and we are together again. I admit, though, I'd love to hear that you missed me."

"Both," I confess, although I no longer need to talk about the things that turned my night into a string of nightmares. Just being here with Alex—his company, his creating the ideal setting—and the nightmares dissolve like the bubbles of foam in my tall glass. The horror of the tattooed number on my arm as my phone number, the terrible insinuation, the shock in the brown eyes at last night's party—all are faint echoes now . . . no longer chafing at my soul.

But Alex must have answers. He pursues the subject in the face of my reluctance. "Don't hesitate to pour your heart out, angel. I know something was troubling you when you called; I could tell. You remember, I've told you: My heart's a radar where you're concerned. It picks up your vibrations. Am I right?"

I cannot avoid Alex's insistent gaze, and begin to talk. I tell him everything that has happened since I saw him last. Alex listens intently, and his eyes turn moist. I put my hand over his lightly.

"Thank you, Alex. For understanding."

"Thank *you*. For trusting me." Alex takes my hand, raises it to his lips, then rising, helps me to my feet. "Let's go for a stroll on the wharf. The air is magnificent, even under an overcast sky."

"I promised Mother that I would be back within an

hour. I'm afraid it's past the deadline. I must get home."

"Will I see you again?"

"I do want to see you," I admit.

I do want to see him, be with him, tell him of my joys and agonies . . . share his triumphs. But can we be together without complications . . . without commitments . . . without arousing my family's objections. Can it be?

"Next Sunday? If that's okay with you."

"Next Sunday . . . But Alex . . . please, no commitments."

The sudden, hearty chuckle, and I know Alex is back in his element. "No commitments; only friendship. Is friendship okay? In your vocabulary, what's the definition of friendship—commitment or no commitment?"

"Friendship is free and open, without constraints . . . without obligations. It's a relationship of give and take, freely offered, freely accepted," I recite as if reading from a dictionary.

"And freely rejected!" Another loud chuckle, and I'm keenly aware of Alex's implication.

"That too."

Alex executes another perfect U-turn in front of our building, pulls alongside the curb, and brings the large car to a standstill. Now he is no longer laughing, and his blue eyes behind the horn-rimmed glasses gaze at me earnestly.

"I accept your terms, Elli, in hopes that in time they will change. I believe they will."

"Alex, you must promise. No pressure."

"It's a deal. No commitments, no pressure. Will I see you next Sunday?"

"Alex, I hope so. But please don't come upstairs now. You see, Mommy has to be prepared . . . I must explain to her . . . I must speak to her alone."

"And you must speak to your brother, and they together must speak to your aunt and uncle. Oh, how I love the Friedman gang! I did miss them. I hope next Sunday I can see them all!"

Chapter Twenty

OUR NEW HOME

"The Friedman Gang," as Alex calls my family, is bustling with excitement when I get home, and not one of them asks a single question about my "date." What's going on? While I was out Uncle Martin returned from the synagogue with exciting news: Mr. Kramer confided to him that a three-room apartment was about to become available in the building, and he promised Uncle to reserve it for Mother and me! My aunt and uncle's building is rent-controlled. The apartments in these buildings are extremely hard to come by, and prospective tenants vie in offering "key money," large sums under the table to managers or superintendents, to have their names placed on waiting lists.

Uncle Martin and dour Mr. Kramer, the landlord, attend the same synagogue, a small, intimate house of worship about a block and a half from our house. The two men regularly meet in the doorway of our building and talk politics along the way. They have developed a friendly regard for each other as they have strolled to and from the evening prayers. Misanthropic Mr. Kramer seems to have grown quite fond of Uncle Martin, to the point where he has actually smiled and returned my greeting when I passed him in the hallway in Uncle's company. It is public knowledge that the elder of Mr. Kramer's two sons, who manages our building, is animated solely by the dynamics of greed, so you can imagine Uncle's surprise this evening when Mr. Kramer drew him aside and hinted that we could have the apartment without money under the table.

"It's nothing short of a miracle!" Aunt Celia exclaims. "How is it possible? I can't believe Kramer Junior will let his father just give the apartment away!"

"I asked him the same question," Uncle Martin reports. "'Don't worry about my son,' he answered. 'I'll take care of it on my end. At your end, you take care that your sister-in-law be ready to move on short notice, perhaps in a day or two. And make sure not to breathe a word to anyone in the meantime,' he warned."

For me the news of the apartment is a double miracle. For the next couple of weeks it occupies center stage and diverts my family's attention from my long telephone conversations and dates with Alex.

My family's preoccupation with Mr. Kramer's news is complicated by not knowing whether the apartment would be available for our occupancy by the beginning of next month or only the following month. It all seems so mysterious, and as time passes, nerve-racking.

One Friday evening as he returns from the synagogue, Uncle Martin's sheepish smile reminds me of my little charges in the orphanage in Bratislava, especially seven-year-old Hesky's mischievous looks whenever he was hiding something. That gives me a clue that Uncle has something up his sleeve. I keep a close watch on Uncle's face all through his chanting the *kiddush*, the sanctification of the wine, his recital of the blessing over the loaves of challah, the white bread, his breaking the bread and handing a portion to each family member. No one else seems to pay attention to the impish, secretive "Hesky look" that does not leave his lips, his features. And only when he has swallowed his portion of the bread and is free to talk do I burst out, "Uncle has good news for us! Let's hear it, Uncle Martin!"

"Whatever gives you that idea?" Uncle pretends annoyance, his face beaming.

"It's the apartment!" I shriek. "I bet it's the apartment."

All eyes focus on Uncle Martin and watch excitement light up his face.

"This devil of a girl has jumped the gun on me again! I wanted to pop the news during dinner. The apartment is vacant, and Kramer wants you to move in by Sunday. . . . Actually he wants you to move Saturday night, during the night so no one in the building would notice."

"Hooray!" I shriek, and jump up to hug Uncle with such vehemence he almost topples over.

"Mazel tov!" Mother shouts. "*Mazel tov.* You did it!"

As soon as I release Uncle from my bear hug, Bubi circles the dining room table to approach him and shake his hand. "Congratulations, Uncle Martin. But what's the intrigue? Why move like thieves in the night?"

"It seems Kramer Junior promised the apartment to other tenants, a young married couple, and they are expected to move in on Monday. But the old man wants us to preempt . . . to present his son with an accomplished fact. Once your mother will have occupied the apartment, young Kramer will have no choice but to accept the inevitable."

"What if finding us occupying the apartment against his wishes, Kramer Junior throws us out?" Mother asks.

"The old man has reassured me that won't happen."

"What about the young couple—where will they go?" I interject.

"It seems the young couple gave Kramer Junior key money weeks ago but didn't move. For some reason they changed their minds. When Kramer Junior refused to return their key money, they resigned themselves to move in. Your preemptive move will, in effect, solve the young couple's problem. Kramer Junior will have no choice but return the key money to the young couple!"

"Sounds like a chess game, Martin, if you ask me," Aunt Celia observes. "I hope your moves will win the game for Laura and Elli."

"Laura is in the fortunate position of having nothing to lose. We'll all pitch in and move over your things, Laurika. We'll carry over the Castro convertible for the two of you to sleep on, a small table, a few chairs, until you buy your own furniture."

"That may take some time," Mother muses.

"We don't need these pieces. Feel free to make use of them as long as it takes."

How long will it take for Mother and me to earn enough money for the furnishings of three rooms and a kitchen? Beds and bed linen, night tables, chests, a dining room table and chairs, a kitchen table and chairs, a couch and a coffee table for the living room, dishes, pots, and pans . . . Who knows when that will happen? It may take a year or more.

"Enough talk," Aunt Celia declares. "Let's eat. We can continue after dinner. After dinner we can discuss the strategy of the move, all the details involved."

During dinner Bubi rises to his feet to make a surprise announcement. His eyes brilliant with repressed excitement, he reveals the existence of a special bank account he opened years ago just for this occasion. He has been saving all these years, working as a waiter in the Catskills during the summers, anticipating the day when Mommy and I would arrive and he would have the funds to furnish our home.

"And now, thank God, that day has arrived," he concludes with a contented smile. "The funds are there for all the furnishings, from A to Z."

I cannot believe my ears. Mother, Aunt, Uncle, and I are stunned into momentary silence, then Mother says, "Bubi, this is truly a surprise. It is very touching. But we must not take the money you saved all these years. It wouldn't be fair. Elli and I, we are working. . . ."

"But this is what I saved it for. The apartment will be also my home—"

"Still. You're a young man. You'll need your savings—"

"Look, Mommy, if it makes you feel better, let's call it a loan. Okay?"

"So it's settled." Uncle Martin raises his glass of Tokay wine. "Here is to the move! And to loyal sons like Bubi! And to a happy new home for all of you, all of us!"

"Amen," Mother says, raising her glass, her voice thick with emotion. "To a new life in America!"

Chapter Twenty-One

THE MOVE!

I have never realized moving could be so thrilling. The cloak-and-dagger operation under the cover of the night of course adds to the excitement.

As Bubi has to return to the yeshiva tonight and cannot help out, I advise that we include the superintendent, Mr. Jackson, in the conspiracy, so he can help us carry the larger pieces—a table, the couch, and even an armchair Aunt Celia insisted we take from her living room. A black man with an impish conspiratorial wink, Mr. Jackson declares that he is "happy to help out, especially to lend a hand to my friend Miss Friedman." A special bond of friendship has developed between Mr. Jackson and me during debates about his proud insistence that the ancient Hebrews were black, a claim that has prompted me to call him my Hebrew Brother.

There is no elevator, and every item taken from my aunt and uncle's apartment has to be maneuvered first one flight down the stairs, then carried noiselessly across the large lobby to the front staircase, and there hauled one flight up the stairs to our new apartment.

Aunt Celia is the lookout. Before each haul she surveys the stairwell and the lobby and signals a warning the very moment she hears someone enter the building. Only after all is quiet do we resume our clandestine moves as swiftly and unobtrusively as possible.

Our footsteps and voices echo in the large, empty rooms. The bedroom is bereft of furniture, while the Castro convertible in one corner of the spacious living and dining room complex and the solitary armchair in the other look a bit forlorn. The kitchen holds a pleasant surprise: The stove, refrigerator, and kitchen cabinets on the walls are integral parts of the apartment! We can immediately put the plates, cutlery, pots, and pans Aunt Celia has given us into the kitchen cupboard. There is even a built-in broom closet in the kitchen! And wonderful walk-in closets in the foyer and the bedroom. We can immediately hang our clothes and place the bed linen and towels Aunt Celia has lent us on the wide, ample shelves.

It's almost 2:00 A.M. when I close the door behind Celia, Martin, and Mr. Jackson, and they tiptoe silently down the corridor, back to their apartments. In our new home all our things are in place.

"Thank God the move has been accomplished, and besides us no one in the building is the wiser." I sigh with relief. "Except, of course, Mr. Kramer Senior."

"And Mr. Kramer Junior will be tomorrow," Mother adds the ominous thought. "And then? All hell will break loose."

"Let's wait and see," I say to calm Mother's frayed

nerves. Mother would have been happier if the move was aboveboard. She does not care for underhanded maneuvers. "All this is too devious for my taste," she kept muttering all night in the heat and haste of the move. "Too deceitful."

"Kramer Junior may not find it out until Monday. Monday you and I are at work. Early Monday morning we are out of the house. We might not even be present when all hell breaks loose. We'll be spared all the excitement, you and I."

"That reminds me. We must not forget to buy a broom on our way home on Monday, and a dustpan."

Of all the non sequiturs, this takes the cake. After all these years I am still amazed at Mother's remarkable capacity to rebound from distress to mundane practicality. I look about me in the bare apartment with its overwhelming emptiness.

"Oh, of course! All we need here is a broom. And a dustpan!"

"Well, take a look. There is litter everywhere. Tomorrow we'll borrow cleaning utensils from Cilike and start scrubbing this place."

"Okay, Mommy." I yawn. "We'll do that tomorrow. But tonight let's go to bed."

Sunday morning Mother's cheerful voice wakes me. True to her word, she has collected all my aunt's sundry cleaning utensils, and the room is cluttered with dust mops and dust rags, huge sponges and pails of water. The dismal scene presents a sharp contrast to Mother's cheerful tone.

"A beautiful winter morning!" Mother cries. "Come to the window. Look!"

With great reluctance I crawl out of my warm nest on the convertible sofa and approach the window. Ocean Avenue has been converted into a winter wonderland! A white blanket of snow covers everything in sight! The bare tree branches that only yesterday were like gray fingers threateningly pointing to the sky are now enormous bouquets of white magnolias, rows and rows of white bouquets lining the street as far as the eye can see.

"How do you like it? The first snowfall in America."

"Beautiful!"

"Doesn't it inspire you to plunge into work, to want to scrub everything as white as snow?"

"That it certainly doesn't. If anything, it inspires me to write a poem."

"I was afraid of that. A poem will not get this house clean. Can you spare some inspiration for cleaning the house, and when it is done use the rest for writing your poem?"

"As if I had a choice!" I laugh at Mother. "The poem will have to play second fiddle. . . ."

Mother and I have a quick breakfast of coffee and toast, and then plunge into work.

I kick off my shoes, hitch my skirt high above my knees with clothespins, and begin mopping operations. The living room done, I begin scrubbing the kitchen floor, when the doorbell rings.

"It must be Celia. She promised to bring some more rags."

I pad through sudsy puddles and open the door to reveal Alex standing in the doorway with a mass of red roses. "Oh, my God! Alex! How did you find us here?"

"Your aunt told me the good news. Congratulations," Alex says, beaming, and hands me a bunch of roses. A second bunch remains cradled in his arm as his glance sweeps from my hair pinned into a bun to my hitched-up skirt and bare feet. "I see you are ready for the concert!"

"The concert . . . Oh, my God, I forgot all about it!"

The noon rehearsal at Carnegie Hall . . . in all the feverish activity it slipped my mind. And Alex is here according to plan at eleven, to take me. Now it's too late. I can't drop everything and leave it to Mother to finish the cleaning all by herself. How can I go to a concert while Mother stays behind to scrub floors? And besides, I will not be able to get ready on time.

"Who's there?" Mother calls from the bathroom.

"Alex is here, Mom."

Mother adjusts the kerchief on her hair and hurries out, smiling. "Hello, Herr Doctor. How did you find us?"

Alex hands Mother the roses. "Congratulations, Frau Friedman. Much luck in your new home."

Mother is pleased. "Thank you. How very gallant of you, Herr Doctor. My favorite flowers—red roses."

Luckily the living room floor is fairly dry, and Mother and I usher Alex to the sofa.

"You're so elegant, Herr Doctor. A special occasion?"

"Alex has come to take me to a concert. Forgive me, Alex, but in all the frenzy of the unexpected move I forgot about our date. . . . And I forgot to let you know. So sorry that we have to miss it."

"When is the concert?" Mother inquires. "Where?"

"At noon. Carnegie Hall, in Manhattan," I answer.

"How long does it take to get there?"

"At this hour on Sunday?" Alex says. "Normally half an hour. Today because of the snow, it may take a bit longer."

"So what's the problem, Elli? Why can't you go? Now it's barely eleven o'clock. How long does it take you to get ready?"

"Frau Friedman, I understand. I don't expect your daughter—under the circumstances—to leave all this and rush off to a concert. Although . . ." Alex turns to me with an amused smile. "I can see Cinderella is dressed for the occasion."

All at once I become fully aware of my hitched-up skirt, bare feet, messy hair.

"Oh, my God! What a sight . . . forgive me . . ." I cry, laughing and hurry to the bathroom. The bathroom mirror reveals my shocking appearance. I quickly wash my face, remove the pins and run a comb through my hair, unclip my skirt, dry my feet, put on a pair of shoes, and rejoin Mother and Alex in the living room.

"Cinderella turned into a princess!" Alex pronounces.

"Alex, forgive me. There's really no time to get ready to go out."

"Come, Elli, don't be so difficult. Get dressed quick, and go to the concert. I'll manage to mop up the rest."

I cast a pleading glance at Alex, and he takes up my

cause. "Frau Friedman, there's no need. We'll take a rain check on the concert."

"Let's have some coffee," I suggest. "The kitchen floor has dried in the meantime."

In one of the cartons I find the percolator we received from Alex, plug it in the outlet, and soon the aroma of coffee perking fills the air. While I set out the coffee cups Mother finds an empty jar and, arranging the roses, places them at the center of the kitchen table.

"I must thank you for this coffee break, Alex," I say. "Mom and I sure needed it."

"I still wish you'd go," Mother pleads. "Herr Doctor, can you make her change her mind?"

Alex laughs. "Don't you know your daughter? If you can't change her mind, nobody can. But I must confess, I'm happier to drink coffee in your new kitchen than listen to a rehearsal at Carnegie Hall."

Chapter Twenty-Two

THE POCONOS

Today I must cut my lunch short at the yeshiva: I'm in a hurry to get to a meeting of my English Conversation Club at Erasmus Hall High. Without waiting for my subway companions, I am flying past the principal's office when I hear the rabbi call after me.

"Miss Friedman, just a moment! Would you step in for a moment?" Oh, no, not today! What can be the matter? Since our last chat when he cautioned me against speaking about the camps, I have been wearing long sleeves to cover the tattooed number on my arm, to avoid answering questions, to avoid any reference to the camps. What can be the matter now?

"Miss Friedman, would you like to work in a summer camp for children and earn some extra money?"

The word *camp* sends a shiver down my spine. "Camp?" I ask, astonished.

Seeing my shock, he hastens to explain, "You see, here during the months of July and August there are recreational programs in the mountains for school children. They call them summer camps. Trained educators work as counselors and teaching staff. You as a teacher are qualified, so I recommended you for the job of counselor in one of the most prestigious summer camps. But, of course, only if you're interested . . ."

Of course I'm interested. To spend the summer in the mountains, and be paid for it! I am very interested. And the rabbi has actually recommended me! I am deeply moved.

"Thank you, Rabbi, for your recommendation. But I'd like to know more about this job. Where's the camp? What does a counselor do? What is the salary?"

"Camp Massad is in Pennsylvania, in the Pocono Mountains. It's a Hebrew-speaking camp; the parents send their children to this camp to learn Hebrew. As a counselor you would be taking care of a group of children, supervise activities, lessons. . . . I don't know the details. If you are interested in the job, I'll set up an appointment for you with the director, Mr. Shlomo Schulsinger. He will give you the exact job description. The salary is not high—I think it's close to a hundred dollars for the summer—but you get tips from parents and they make up the bulk of the pay. If you want, I can call him right now. They are hiring now. . . . As a matter of fact, I hope it's not too late."

"Thank you very much. Yes, I believe . . . please call him now . . . if you don't mind."

I glance at my watch. My meeting! The rabbi picks up the telephone receiver, and I walk out into the outer office and there I wait anxiously while the murmur of the conversation drones on.

"Miss Friedman." The rabbi beams when I reenter his office. "We are lucky. We secured the very last position as counselor. He wants to see you today. You can go there straight from here. The offices of the *Histadrut* that runs the camp are in downtown Manhattan; it's on your way home to Brooklyn. . . ."

"I'm sorry, today I can't. I must hurry to a meeting. Can the appointment be changed for Wednesday?"

Rabbi Charney calls again and, still holding the receiver, nods in my direction. "Wednesday's fine. At three o'clock?"

"Three o'clock is fine, thank you." I nod back.

Mr. Schulsinger is a man of few words. On Wednesday at 3:00 P.M. sharp I enter his office, and at 3:15 sharp I exit his office, hired as a counselor in Camp Massad Aleph in Pennsylvania, starting in little more than a month.

Preparations for camp are exciting, overwhelming, and expensive. I am given a list of things to buy and an exact number in each category—two pairs of long trousers, two pairs of shorts; six undershirts; six T-shirts; six bath, six facial, and six hand towels; four pillow cases; four fitted and four flat sheets; eight pairs of heavy socks; one pair of boots; two pairs of tennis shoes; three sweaters; four sweatshirts; two duffel bags. . . . What are sweatshirts? What's a duffel bag? I am instructed to have name tags printed with my name and sewn into every item of clothing and bedding!

Summer heat grips the city with a fiery fist. Sweat pours down my face as I am stitching name tags into woolen blankets, into warm trousers, sweaters, heavy sweatshirts. . . . This is insane, all these winter clothes. Are we preparing to spend the summer in Alaska? But Bubi knows better. The Poconos are high mountains, he says; it gets quite cold there in the evening. I still can't believe it. I still think someone in the camp management must have gone mad and made an outrageous mistake, but I keep stitching and mopping my brow. The duffel bags have to be ready for pickup on June 20, five days before departure for camp.

On the last day of school my little first-graders have a surprise for me. Two representatives of the class, a girl and a boy, with glowing faces, present me with a large box wrapped in shiny pink paper.

"Open it! Open it!" The class chants, and I unwrap the box, carefully saving the shiny wrapping paper. The class holds its breath as I open the box and remove layers of tissue paper, exposing a colorful ceramic fruit bowl. When I lift the bowl out of the box, the class cheers and applauds.

"It's beautiful!" I exclaim, and pass among the rows, hugging each girl and boy. "Thank you, thank you, thank you. . . ."

I write the address of Camp Massad on the blackboard, and all the children promise to write me letters during the summer, and I promise to respond to each.

"Children, don't forget to write your own address on the back of the envelope. So I can write back to you."

Promises, good-byes, and hugs, and the school day is over, the school year is over. My first school year in America. The first year of my American teaching career.

I love these children and don't want to part with

them. Will I see them again? I have been hired to teach here next September, a new first grade. These children will be here, attending second grade. Of course I will see them. And yet it will not be the same. . . . They will not be my children then; they will belong to another classroom, another teacher, and I will have another group of first-graders to love.

"*Shalom,* children. Don't forget to write!"

Tomorrow I leave for camp. This is the first time ever that Mother and I will be separated for two months. A searing emptiness gnaws at my insides.

"Two months is a long time," I say heavily when we are ready for bed.

"Stop fretting. We'll write to each other," Mother admonishes. "I'll tell you all about my days in detail. Maybe Celia and I will take a short vacation and come to visit you."

"Will you?" I hug her neck. "Will you really?"

"Yes, we've already discussed it. Wanted to surprise you . . . but since you seem so downcast, I decided to tell you now."

"Thank you, Mom. That's simply wonderful! When will you come?"

"On visiting day. That's in about four weeks. We'll find out the bus schedule. We'll come with an early bus, and spend the day with you in camp."

It takes a long time to fall asleep as I anticipate the summer, the camp with other young people, with children, the mountains, and to top it all, my mother and my aunt's visit.

Chapter Twenty-Three

CAMP MASSAD

At first glance the camp, the forest clearing framed by barracklike structures facing a flagpole at its center, reminds me of a military compound. The forest, like a verdant blanket, wraps itself around the clearing and the barracks as if to insulate them from the lure of the mountains, the fabulous Poconos beckoning far ahead, towering and expectant.

At the bottom of the hill a lake shimmers, an icy blue, forbidding threshold to another foothill on its far side that accommodates another circle of barracklike structures around a flagpole—the boys' camp. This is Camp Massad Aleph in the Pocono Mountains.

The children in both camps are assembled in five age groups, each division identified with a metaphorical tree section, beginning with Root, or *Shoresh* in Hebrew, the youngest, and rising in age ever higher to Trunk *(Geza)*, to Branch *(Anaf)* and Blossom *(Nitzan)*, culminating in the top, called Crown *(Tzameret)*.

I am assigned to a bunk in *Shoresh*, the division comprising about fifty children ranging from six to eight years old. Seven beds are in my bunk, one of regular size and six small ones for my little five- to six-year-old campers whose round-the-clock care is my charge. I am responsible for their daily activities—getting up in the morning, getting ready for roll call, getting to the dining room for breakfast, to the sport field for morning activity, to the dining room for lunch, back to the bunk for rest period, to the recreation room for study period, to the field for afternoon activity, to the dining room for dinner, to the lawn for evening activity, to the showers an hour before curfew, and to bed before lights-out—on the dot. During meals I'm responsible for their proper conduct; during rest period for quiet; during activities for their proper attire depending on the time of day; at curfew, their orderly preparations for bedtime; and after lights-out for total silence in the bunk.

On the first day I meet my tender little *Shorashim,* six little girls intimidated by their strange new surroundings and terrified by their distance from home. I embrace them and hold them close, ask about their pets, their favorite hobbies, encourage them to divulge their favorite nicknames, and finally tell them bedtime stories until they fall asleep.

The next morning the harsh reality of the tight daily schedule hits me like an ice-cold shower. I must assume the role of drill sergeant to get my charges to meet the schedule's demands. When my bunk appears several minutes late for roll call, all eyes are on the six little sleepyheads and their red-faced counselor, and when we bring up the rear on line for breakfast, we incur the dismayed looks of the kitchen staff. I learn my lesson: No matter how impossible it seems, it must be done; it is up to me to have my little charges move from activity to activity with clocklike precision!

How do you combine a drill sergeant's discipline with maternal indulgence?

Most of the other counselors, girls and boys my age, seem to know the secret; they have done this before. Even before working as counselors, most were campers in Massad, then CITs (counselors in training) and assistant counselors. They know each other from previous summers, and their circle of familiarity seems impenetrable.

Summer camps, I come to recognize, are closed societies. Members follow older siblings as campers, then staff, and the exclusive circle is perpetuated ad infinitum. How can I, an outsider, make inroads into the circle?

Once I know the reason, I find my exclusion from the circle easier to bear. The crushing sense of loneliness, the almost devastating sense of being "the other" brings back painful memories. Never since my arrival in America have I had such a palpable sensation of not belonging.

Only on nights when we sit around the campfire and sing Hebrew songs to the accompaniment of a single guitar, swaying to the melody with arms locked, does my loneliness subside. Instead a powerful yearning takes hold of my soul. As if a primal memory, an uncanny recollection, stirred, my soul rises above the leaping flames of the campfire and, spanning the expanse of time and space, reunites with the soul of my biblical namesake, Leah, to

roam the landscape of my ancient-new homeland—
biblical-modern Israel.

"I've noticed," Oded the guitar player addresses me
one night as the singing breaks up and we begin our trek
through the woods toward the camp, "whenever we sing
around the camp fire, your face has a special glow. Are
you from Israel?"

"No. But I wish I were."

"Why?"

"I love Israel."

"Have you ever been to Israel?"

"No. Never. But I so wished to go there after libera-
tion from the camps . . . with the first transports. Have
you? Ever been to Israel?"

"I am from Israel. I was born there. I just came here
for the summer."

"Really? I've never met anyone from Israel. I've never
even met anyone who visited Israel. Where in Israel
where you born?"

"In Tel Aviv."

I want to know everything about Tel Aviv, about
Israel, the cities, the mountains, the desert. . . . I don't
know where to begin. But Oded does not wait for my
questions; he begins to talk about Tel Aviv and its beautiful beach on the Mediterranean, about the hills and the
Sea of Galilee, about Jerusalem. In the meantime we
emerge into the clearing and reach my bunk. Oded waits
outside while I tiptoe into my room to check on the
sleeping children, and then the two of us sit on the stoop
of the bungalow and talk late into the night.

"Oh, God, it's past midnight!" Oded exclaims. "I must be in my bunk. *Layla Tov,* Leah. See you in the morning!"

In Camp Massad we call each other by our Hebrew names. Leah is my Hebrew name, the name of one of our biblical matriarchs.

"*Layla Tov,* Oded." I watch his slim, medium frame, his guitar slung on one shoulder, disappear into the shadows, and I make my way quietly into my bunk. Lying in bed I recall every one of Oded's tales about Israel, and slowly, imperceptibly, a dream takes shape, a newborn hope fills the nagging emptiness and lulls me to sleep.

Oded becomes a special friend. At the campfire he insists the *haverim* reserve a seat near me, and when he begins to play the guitar he turns in my direction as if dedicating the melody to our common love of Israel.

I learn to dance the *hora,* the spirited dance of the pioneers in Israel. We dance with arms locked around the campfire, as if the songs Oded plays on his guitar take wing. The circle of dancers soars ever faster around and around, molding into a solid swirling ring. And I too soar; I too become one with the circle.

I love to dance. And the *hora* is not merely a dance; it is a confession of age-old yearnings, a declaration of love.

I suppose because of his guitar playing, Oded is one of the most popular boys in camp, and his attentions to me do not pass unnoticed. Some of the girls drop wide hints about Oded and me being a couple, and make no secret of their curiosity.

"What is there to tell?" I respond with a question to a list of probing questions. I can understand the girls' curiosity. There is fierce competition for the cute guys and Oded is one of them, but I resent the prying. "We are friends. He plays the guitar, and we sing together. Oded loves to talk about his homeland, and I love to listen."

At first I'm offended by my fellow counselors' intrusive questions, their giggling. Oded's friendship is too precious to be tarnished by snickering and gossip. Eventually the questions stop, my relationship with Oded slips into the comfortable realm of the routine, and I am relieved.

It's a scorching Thursday afternoon. The second week of camp is drawing to an end. My tired campers, Yael, Michal, Adina, Laura, Daniela, and Shulamit, are dragging their feet as we climb the hill from the dining room to the bunk for our rest period.

In the distance I spot two people, a young woman of medium height in a blue blouse and white shorts and a tall young man wearing long slacks, a wide-rimmed hat, waiting under the acacia tree near our bunk. As we come nearer I recognize them: It's my brother and his girl-friend, Evelyn!

"What a surprise!" I shriek, and, forgetting to act like a grown-up in front of my charges, rush to hug them. "What a surprise! I didn't know you were coming! Why didn't you write?"

"If we did, it wouldn't be a surprise," my brother says with typical Bubiesque logic.

My joy knows no bounds. Seeing my brother makes me realize how much I have missed him, how homesick I have been. How good it is to see them both looking so well, so happy.

My little campers are excited with the unexpected visit of my brother and his girlfriend, and want to know everything about them—their names, their ages, and when they will get married.

Evelyn, Bubi, and I burst into spontaneous laughter.

"No more questions," I announce in order to extricate the three of us from the awkward moment. "We are late for rest period." I usher my little herd of smart alecks into the bunk and ask them to cooperate by hopping into bed in record time so I can join my guests.

I spread a blanket under the shady tree, and from a large paper bag Evelyn produces a bunch of grapes and a box of cookies.

"My grandmother baked these for you," she says with a smile. "They are good."

"Oh, thank you."

"Wait, this is not all." Bubi rummages in the bag. "Mom sends you—guess what! *Makos pogacsa.*" The chewy Hungarian pastry with poppy seeds has been my all-time favorite.

"Thank you both so much for this happy surprise . . . for bringing me a bit of home."

As we begin to nibble on the home-baked goodies, I tell them about my camp experiences and impressions, and they tell me about home, about the terrific heat wave in New York, and how Mom, Aunt Celia, and Uncle Martin cope. Then Evelyn casts a meaningful glance at my brother.

"I was tempted to answer that little kid's question about getting married," she says, blushing. "Do you want to know the answer?"

"Of course!" I yell, once again losing my composure. "Of course!"

"I guess sometime at the end of the year . . . in December. We'll wait with the engagement party until you come home."

"*Mazel tov!* Congratulations!" I scream, and lose control of my emotions altogether, sobbing and laughing simultaneously.

Evelyn and Bubi rise; they must leave now in order to make the three o'clock bus, the last one back to New York. I walk with them to the gate of the camp, and my heart dances along.

Chapter Twenty-Four

YISHAI

There is a cold wind tonight, and Oded offers his jacket as we make our way back to camp. Bubi and Evelyn's news has put me in a giddy mood, and I accept Oded's jacket with a playful flourish. "Thank you, Sir Galahad," I say expansively. "I'm honored to wear the garment that has touched your gallant shoulders."

Oded is infected by my happy mood, and when I shiver visibly despite his heavy jacket, in imitation of my playful tone he asks, "Tonight is going to be a very cold night, Leah. Do you want me to come and keep you warm in your bed?"

"Of course. What a splendid idea," I say, laughing.

Oded gives my hand a light squeeze: "At twelve thirty, then!" He is now laughing, as well. "*Shalom. Lehitraot.* So long."

"Brilliant sense of humor, Oded! *Shalom. Layla Tov.* Good night!" I call after him, pleased with the little flirtation between us.

I am awakened by the light touch of fingers fondling my hair, caressing my face. Oded is leaning over me, and in the next instant his lips reach my lips. I sit up in alarm.

"What are you doing here?"

"Shh, don't raise your voice, for God's sake. You'll wake the children," he whispers.

"Oded, what are you doing here?"

"You forgot? You told me to come. You invited me to keep you warm in bed. It's twelve thirty."

"But that was a joke. We were joking . . . ," I say, and begin to shiver.

"Joking? Some joke!" Oded is livid. In the pale, clear moonlight streaming into the room I can see his fair skin has flushed scarlet. "You invite me to your bed and you call that a joke? What's the matter with you? How can you do this to me? I climb up the hill on this cold night, all the way from the boys' camp, and you change your mind just like that? What are you—a tease? There's a name for girls like you. . . ." Oded's voice is a sharp hiss. He begins to back out of the room.

"I'm sorry, Oded. I really thought you were joking."

"There's one thing you can do. Don't breathe a word to anyone about this."

"I promise. If you won't, I won't."

The door closes behind him, and my head goes into a spin, whipping up a wave of nausea. How did this come about? How could such misunderstanding happen? How could Oded think that I actually invited him to my bed? What kind of girl would invite a guy to her bed in one room with six little children? How could he assume such a thing?

Was I wrong to assume that Oded knew me? Was I

naive or silly to believe our friendship was genuine? What did Oded call me . . . a tease? And what is the name for girls like me? He didn't say.

Oded is true to his word: This morning no one seems to know of last night's terrible fiasco. Even Ron and Dov, Oded's closest friends, treat me with warmth, as if nothing happened between Oded and me. And the girls continue to treat me with grudging admiration, unaware that my "affair" with Oded is over.

I am the only one aware that Oded studiously avoids my presence, and when he inadvertently meets me his face is frozen with fury. It is very painful to deal with Oded's anger, the way his boyish features twist into a grimace, and even his blond curls seem to stiffen when he sees me. Can this anger ever be assuaged? Will we ever be able to talk as before?

Ever since the agonizing episode with Oded I have been suffering from nausea and sudden stabs of abdominal pain. This morning the pain is so severe, I am unable to take my campers to the dining room for breakfast. Miriam, my next-door neighbor, volunteers to gather my flock under her wings until I feel better.

"I'll ask Dr. Zeev, the camp physician, to come up here and check you out," Miriam proposes, but I dismiss the notion.

"There's no need to make a fuss. I'll rest a while and I'll be fine."

Thankfully Miriam ignores my objection, and Dr.

Zeev arrives in about fifteen minutes. By the time he reaches the bunk, my pain is excruciating. The doctor calls for the camp transport to take me to the emergency room at the hospital in Stroudsburg. Yishai, the camp general secretary, helps the driver carry me on a stretcher to the station wagon, and to my surprise accompanies me to the hospital. On the two-hour drive to Stroudsburg, my severe pain is eased by Yishai's soothing voice and his gentle touch on my hand.

Yishai does not stir from my side while we wait in the emergency room for our turn, and when the attending physician's examination is over, Yishai approaches him to inquire about my condition.

"What's the diagnosis, Doctor?" he asks with the genuine concern of an older brother.

When the doctor reveals the diagnosis as severe gall bladder infection and recommends hospitalization, Yishai requests permission to accompany me to my room. After I am put to bed and hooked up to the intravenous tube, he sits at my bedside until the painkiller takes effect and the pain subsides. Only then does he take his leave, and promises to return during visiting hours tomorrow.

All evening I find myself thinking about the tall, slim camp VIP who accompanied me to the hospital and stayed with me, easing my pain and alarm. I keep remembering his large brown eyes, the gap between his two front teeth, his prominent ears, his long neck, and I offer a silent prayer: *Please God, make Yishai keep his word.*

At the onset of visiting hours, at 1:00 P.M., Yishai arrives with the first batch of visitors. When I see his tan, smiling face appear in the doorway of the hospital ward, my heart skips a beat.

"I brought you a present," Yishai declares with a secretive smile, and from a large brown paper bag he draws a white sweatshirt emblazoned with the camp's name and emblem. "It's long enough for a nightshirt, you can wear it instead of the hospital gown!"

"Oh, thank you, Yishai. How thoughtful."

"This is not all. Miriam packed up your toothbrush, hairbrush, and the like. And this." Yishai hands over a large manila envelope stuffed with *Life* magazines and a small white envelope bulging with bits of paper. "The magazines are courtesy of the camp management. And these are decorated love letters. Your campers drew them. And they send you lots of good wishes for a speedy recovery."

Some twenty pieces of paper, mostly drawings, and a letter from Miriam. I place it all in the drawer; will read it all later, after Yishai's visit.

"We did not notify your family. We wanted to consult you first."

"Thank you, Yishai. No need to let them know. My mother would worry unnecessarily. As is, I may be discharged in a day or two."

Before we know it, visiting hours are over. All the visitors must leave the ward without delay.

"Tomorrow we have field trips—I may not be able to come. I'll try. If I can't, I'll make sure someone else will."

When Yishai leaves, the ward seems dull, colorless. The white metal drawer creaks as I open it and take out first the children's drawings—hearts, flowers, hospital beds, smiling faces, all spelling love—and then Miriam's letter. Miriam's letter is full of news. All the counselors in *Shoresh* are taking turns to care for my campers, all send their best wishes, expressions of concern ... affection. My heart overflows. It was only three weeks ago that I felt like an outsider. . . .

On the morning rounds the attending physician informs me that my temperature has gone down and I will be discharged today. Great news! But how do I get back to camp? Would he please notify the camp administration? The doctor nods, and within minutes a nurse comes to my bed with the news: "Please be ready to be picked up at twelve noon."

Hadassah, the camp nurse, and Sarah, the girls' head counselor, come along with the driver to take me "home." My campers rush out to greet me. They wrap themselves around my legs and pull at my arms. Luckily it's the rest period and we can all climb into bed, and in a low whisper I tell them stories until all of us fall asleep.

In the evening a surprise awaits me. I find out that Yishai's present, the sweatshirt emblazoned with the camp's emblem, was a sort of declaration, a symbol of his claim. At dinner Yishai, wearing the same sweatshirt, approaches my table.

"Welcome home, Leah. We're all happy you're back," he says, the wide-open smile showing the gap in his front teeth and emphasizing the dimple in his left cheek. Then the smile fades and his face turns serious. "Leah, the sweatshirt I gave you . . . I thought you'd be wearing it tonight. You see, it's a special shirt, only for members of the administration. When people will see you wear it . . . both of us at the same time, everyone will know . . ." His attention is caught by some activity in the middle of the dining room, and he hurries off without finishing the sentence.

I am puzzled. What does this all mean? Later in the evening I seek out Miriam, or Miri, as she prefers to be called. She is an "old-timer" here in camp; she'll perhaps be able to explain.

Miri laughs. "It's obvious. When a boy and a girl show up in identical sweatshirts, it's as good as an official announcement. You're now expected to wear that sweatshirt every morning to roll call and breakfast, and every evening to dinner to let the whole camp know that Yishai and you are a couple."

"Yishai and me—a couple? When did that happen? How?"

"Don't you know? When did Yishai give you the sweatshirt?'

"He brought it to the hospital. He said I should wear it as a hospital gown. I didn't know it meant more than that!"

"Well, now you know. . . ." Miri laughs again.

"It's as simple as that? A boy gives you one of his sweatshirts and that sets you up? And what if you don't feel the same way about it?"

"Then you don't accept the shirt. That's his answer. You accepted his offer when you took his shirt and put it on."

So Yishai and I are a couple. I am thrilled and troubled at the same time. I like Yishai, I like him very much. I believe I'm falling in love with him because of his kindness to me in the hospital, his gentle, caring attitude. Am I a fool? Why do I turn into a foolish, defenseless child whenever someone shows tenderness to me?

Yishai being my boyfriend is a matter of incredible prestige. And yet this public display of a very private feeling is somehow wrong. I feel my personal life has been invaded. Publicly parading my relationship with Yishai somehow cheapens it. The longer I think about it the more I am convinced that I do not want to go along with it.

Luckily I am still on sick rest, and do not have to confront this issue face-to-face quite yet. I am excused from roll call and early breakfast, Miriam and Hadassah look after my campers for the next few days, and by lunchtime it's much too hot to wear a sweatshirt. At dinnertime when I appear in my own lavender sweatshirt, I brace myself for a confrontation with Yishai. What kind of confrontation will it be? Will I be able to explain it to him? Or will he be too hurt, too upset to listen?

Yishai is not in the dining room—must be attending to some administrative affair—and I sigh with relief. The issue is postponed for one more day. The next evening Yishai is much too busy; he barely has time to come over to our table for a quick *Shalom*-how-are-you. But after dinner he waits for me at the entrance. Here it comes— the confrontation.

"There's a hike tomorrow night after curfew, for all

the counselors," he says in a hurry. "It will be announced tomorrow morning at roll call. I'll be away all day tomorrow, but wanted to know, can you come on the hike?"

"I hope so . . . I will."

A dimply smile brightens Yishai's tan face, and he is gone, leaving me with an exciting, secret anticipation of tomorrow evening. I march my campers to evening activity, and then help them get ready for bed.

The hike is an annual night activity for the staff, and from the excited preparations that go on all day it seems it is the high point of the summer. The kitchen staff is preparing food for a picnic and all kinds of goodies for roasting at the campfire—frankfurters, potatoes, and other tidbits I am not familiar with, white and pink fluffy balls Miriam calls marshmallows. We are told to prepare drinks in our canteens, wear warm sweaters and slacks, and bring along blankets.

After curfew the senior staff takes over supervision of the campers and we counselors, boys and girls, about sixty of us, gather near the flagpole and begin the hike by marching out of the camp, through the woods, into the nearby mountains. It is a wonderful night. The mountain breeze seems to carry us up and up on the steep mountain trail toward the starry, moonlit sky. Boys and girls pair up, and I am looking for Yishai. Didn't he come? Last-minute camp business must have detained him.

The climb gradually slows to a halt, we reach a plateau, and all at once I sense a light touch on my shoulder. It's Yishai.

Now Yishai is in full charge, giving instructions to the

boys on preparing the campfire, and to the girls on readying the picnic on the blankets. Soon the sound of singing rises from around the campfire. The roasted potatoes are delicious, the franks are better than anything I have ever tasted, and the toasted marshmallows are gone before I have a chance to taste one.

Yishai reappears, and in his palm are three browned marshmallows. "I saved some marshmallows for you. I saw you didn't get any."

"Thank you. Let me taste just one. . . ."

I do not really care for the consistency but swallow it anyway out of gratitude for Yishai's kindness.

"You don't like it, I can tell," Yishai laughs.

Oded plays his guitar, and we sing popular Hebrew songs to the accompaniment of crackling fire, and the breeze carries the melody on the wings of fiery sparks. We are a swaying circle, all sixty-odd of us, fluid, harmonious . . . one. How I wish this night would never end, the magic would last forever.

Slowly the cinders die out and we all rise to tidy up the grounds, still singing, the music from Oded's guitar still reverberating as, arms locked, we make our way down the hill in the direction of the camp. It is an exhilaratingly fast downhill walk under the fabulous night sky. Yishai is at my side now and we march together, our breathing in rhythmic spurts in time to the beating of my heart. At the bottom of the hill the trail leads to a clearing in the woods. As if on cue, one couple after another strays across the clearing and disappears among the bushes.

"Where is everyone going?" I ask Yishai in astonishment.

"To the bushes," he replies, his voice matter-of-fact. "Do you want to come?"

"What do you mean?"

"I mean, do you want to come with me to the bushes? Don't worry, no one will see us. There's plenty of bushes for everyone. . . ."

I struggle to produce a sound.

"Yishai . . ." I gulp. "I am going back to camp, to the bunk. It's been a long night. Are you coming along?"

"I'll stay around here a for a while. *Shalom*, Leah. *Layla tov.*"

"*Layla tov.*" I wave, and join a few stragglers on the trail back to camp.

Chapter Twenty-Five

CULTURE SHOCK

At breakfast Yishai approaches my table, and the inscrutable smile on his face makes my heart sink. Is he coming to explain last night, his abrupt good-bye, his not even walking me to the gate of the camp?

"Leah, I have a favor to ask you." He leans over so the others won't hear. "Would you mind returning my sweatshirt?"

"Your sweatshirt? But I thought it was a present."

"You aren't wearing it anyway."

I feel the blood rush to my face. "I *have* been wearing it. . . ." My stomach feels as if someone has wrung it like a wet rag. Not a word of explanation about last night, and now this? "But if you want it back, I'll bring it at lunchtime."

At lunchtime I do not spot Yishai at first, but later on he passes my table, barely glancing in my direction.

"Thank you," he says simply when I hand him the paper bag containing the sweatshirt. He hangs back for a moment. "Leah, I forgot to ask, how do you feel? Are you fully recovered?"

"Yes, I'm fully recovered. Thank you. I feel perfectly fine."

"I am glad, truly glad."

"And I am truly glad to know that you are truly glad." I laugh.

Yishai laughs too.

"Leah, you're always so much fun to be with!" he says as he walks away, carrying the sweatshirt in the bag.

This cannot be the last chapter in the sweatshirt saga. I must have it out with Yishai. We must have a frank talk and find out what has gone wrong between us. After all, it was Yishai who singled me out and made all the overtures from the very beginning. It was *he* who chose to accompany me to the hospital and behave like a big brother, making me feel so cherished. I came to believe that he cared for me and felt so proud when he spread the news about our relationship and wanted me to wear his sweatshirt, for all to see. I was thrilled seeing his eagerness when he invited me to come along on the hike. I felt our relationship was reaching a high point. What happened? Why did it all change?

Perhaps it is not too late. I'm not giving up. I'm willing to swallow my pride and confront him directly. Tonight right after putting my campers to bed I will search him out and explain how bad and confused I feel about our misunderstanding, and demand answers. I must have answers. This not knowing I find unbearable.

At dinnertime something happens that stuns me into canceling my plans. As the group of young CITs, counselors in training, files out of the dining room, I spot one of them wearing Yishai's sweatshirt. It is unmistakably his white sweatshirt emblazoned with the camp's name and emblem, and buxom Beth is wearing it!

Beth! How did she get it? There must be some mistake. Did Yishai give the sweatshirt to Beth right after I returned it to him? How can I find out? And yet I dare not ask either Beth or Yishai. What if the answer is yes?

I must talk to someone or I'll go mad. Miriam is the one. I feel I can confide in her. She seems mature and sensitive; she'll understand my predicament.

I can barely wait for my campers to fall asleep. Finally their rhythmic breathing provides the signal that I can go over to the next bunk.

I find Miriam sitting at the narrow wooden desk, writing.

"I am sorry to interrupt you, Miri. But I must talk to you."

"No problem. It's only a letter." Miriam nods, and with characteristic calm pushes her chair back and rises. "Let's sit on the stoop. We can talk out there."

The heavy silence of the dark woods stills my anguish, helps to unburden my soul and to divulge my dismal failures—the fiasco with Oded and the devastating finale of my involvement with Yishai.

Miriam listens quietly, and when I am finished she puts her arm about me.

"Leah, don't you know what's going on around you? If you don't you know what *going to the bushes* means, I'll spell it out for you. *Going to the bushes* means having sex. By refusing to go to the bushes with Yishai, you rejected him. So naturally he wanted his sweatshirt back. He wanted to give it to the girl who did go to the bushes with him."

"Beth? To the bushes? But she is no more than fifteen! And Yishai is twenty-four, a grown man; he would never do a thing like that with a fifteen-year-old girl! Miri, it is not possible."

"In America fifteen is not a child when it comes to sex. And everyone knows that Beth has had a crush on him ever since she was a camper. So when you rejected him, when you offended his manhood by not wearing the sweatshirt and then by not going to the bushes with him, he took her, the infatuated girl, to the bushes. So he wanted his sweatshirt back, to give it to her. It is as simple as that."

"Simple? How can you say that?"

"Leah, where have you been all these years? Haven't you learned about the birds and the bees? You should feel flattered that Yishai gave you the sweatshirt before you went to the bushes with him. It's usually done the other way around."

"It's not that I don't know about sex. I have known about sex ever since I was ten, or younger. But I grew up believing sex was—don't laugh at me, but I believe sex is sacred and should be saved for marriage. In my home-town girls were ostracized if they slept around. Even boys were held to task if they did not act responsibly, if they did not treat a girl with proper respect."

"Leah, I want you to come back here in an hour after the curfew, when all the lights are out. We will stay by the window and watch. Then maybe you'll understand."

Just as Miriam instructed, I wait till lights out, and then I make my way in the darkness to her bunk. Miriam draws two chairs to her window and we take up our positions. We sit still, peering into the night, waiting.

I begin to discern one shadowy figure after another emerging from the bunks and moving across the square toward the bushes at the far end. I recognize them, the nicest girls, and there in the distance, near the bushes, I can make out silhouettes of boys, waiting.... One by one they pair up and disappear among the dark foliage of the woods.

"Now that you have seen it with your own eyes . . . now you believe me?" Miriam asks, not in triumph but with profound sympathy. "The sooner you accept the world as it is the sooner you'll learn to be part of it, and to stop castigating yourself."

"How about you, Miri? Why aren't you out there in the bushes like all the others?"

"Not *all* the others. There are quite a few who are not out there. It's a matter of choice. I choose not to. But I'm not devastated by the fact that others do."

It's past midnight. I am ready to return to my bunk.

"Are you leaving already? If you wait a bit longer you'll see your friend Oded with Karen . . . and even Yishai with Beth."

"Thank you, I've seen enough."

Thoroughly shaken, I make my way back to my bunk, thinking of all the other bunks left unsupervised. What if, feeling ill or frightened, one of the little campers calls for

help and the counselor is not there? The thought fills me
with dismay.

Thank God tomorrow is visiting day. I was able to
arrange a ride for Mommy and Aunt Celia with one of
my camper's parents who live in our neighborhood. I
can't wait to see Mommy and Aunt Celia, to hug them,
talk to them, and regain my perspective.

All morning my campers and I are excited with the
anticipation of our guests' arrival. Soon the grounds ring
with the cheerful cries of reunion between the campers
and their parents. My camper's parents arrive, and
Mommy is with them. She is approaching, her face radi-
ant with joy, her arms open for an embrace.

"Mommy! How great to see you," I shout as I run to
meet her. "Did you have a good journey? Where's Aunt
Celia?"

"She couldn't come," Mother says guardedly as we
chat within earshot of my campers' parents. "Mr. Brand
had no room in the car. . . . Mrs. Brand's parents decided
to come along."

I am ready to cry out with disappointment but must
hide it so as not to offend the Brands. After all, they did
give a lift to Mom.

"Celia was very disappointed, but it couldn't be
helped. With God's help you'll be home in less than three
weeks, and you'll see each other then. Celia sends her
love." Mother adds with a wink, "And a loaf of chocolate
cake."

Mother is delighted with the camp: She loves the

crisp, clean mountain air, the woods, the rolling hills. As soon as all my campers are reunited with their parents, I feel free to take Mother for a walk. We go down to the lake, spread a blanket in the shade of the reeds, and reminisce about our summer in the Carpathians.

By the time Mother and I return to camp, walking arm in arm, and Mother joins the Brands on the return trip to New York, a sense of contentment has replaced yesterday's heavy gloom.

Three weeks pass quickly, and soon camp is over. The farewell party, picture taking, hugs and kisses, and the promises of get-togethers, turn the last day of camp into a virtual moment of love. Even Oded makes a half-hearted apology.

Yishai hands me an envelope. It contains a poem. It is a love poem in Hebrew, a lighthearted, somewhat humorous poem and yet it manages to convey intense feeling, deep regret.

When we meet a little later, Yishai's face is grave and his eyes are wistful. "Will I see you in the city?"

"I don't know, Yishai."

"Will you come to the reunion?"

Two hands clasp my shoulders from behind and I turn to face Sarah, the head counselor, who locks me in a tight embrace. "Leah, I am so sorry that we didn't spend more time together," she says warmly. "That we didn't get to know each other better. I am sure we would've found so much to talk about. Perhaps we'll meet in the city? What do you say?"

"Perhaps," I say, slightly overwhelmed. She is the third

person to say the very same words to me today.

Shoshanah, the camp mother, approaches and plants a warm kiss on my forehead. Hillel, the poet, throws his arms about me from behind. Zeev, the camp doctor, and Eliezer, the camp rabbi, come to shake hands.

By the time I am free to turn back to him, Yishai is gone.

Chapter Twenty-Six

A CHANCE MEETING

It's late Friday afternoon, barely enough time to reach home before the Sabbath. Leslie and I race down the ramp at Times Square Station in a dead heat to catch the Brighton train bound for Brooklyn. We lingered too long at Professor Kutscher's talk on the Dead Sea Scrolls, waiting for a chance to talk to the prominent scholar from Jerusalem after the lecture.

The train is packed as usual, but the two of us manage to squeeze into seats next to each other and launch into our discussion of the lecture. Leslie shares my fascination with the ancient scrolls discovered rather recently in a cave near Khirbat Qumran by a shepherd chasing after a stray lamb.

Oded and Yishai and Camp Massad are a distant memory.

A new teacher at the Yeshiva of Central Queens, Leslie Beck also lives in Brooklyn, and it was he who suggested we attend the Friday-afternoon lecture series at the Hebrew Teachers' Association together. And so from the beginning of the school year the two of us have greatly enjoyed the talks and our discussions on the homebound train.

"I find *The Manual of Discipline* the most fun among the scrolls," Leslie begins. "And I think so does Professor Kutscher. It is more interesting than *The Isaiah Scroll*. Do you agree?"

"For me it is interesting because I'm interested in early Christianity, and in the Essenes. The *Manual* sheds light on their lifestyle."

"Did you know that Jesus was an Essene?" Leslie asks excitedly.

From the corner of my eye I notice a tall, dark man making his way in our direction from the other end of the crowded subway car. I become fully aware of him only when, like the Tower of Pisa, he leans above us at a slant, eavesdropping on our conversation.

Suddenly he bends down so low, his face is almost touching mine. "Forgive me, but am I right in believing that you are conversing in Hebrew?" he asks in English, a somewhat embarrassed smile matching his meticulous formality.

I am startled. My answer is halting, deliberately hesitant. "Yes . . . it is Hebrew."

"I hoped it would be. That's why I came all the way over here. Just to hear Hebrew spoken. I hope you don't mind."

Leslie charitably reassures him that we do not mind, and to my annoyance the young man with charcoal eyes remains hanging above our heads and continues to listen to our conversation.

Prospect Park is Leslie's destination, and as Leslie prepares to exit the train, the stranger turns to me and asks in impeccable Hebrew, "May I take your companion's vacated seat next to you?"

Who is this fellow with his mysterious dark looks, extravagant politeness, and unmatched, almost biblical, eloquence?

I nod, and the stranger slides his large frame into the narrow space with surprising agility.

Once seated, to my astonishment he picks up the thread of discussion interrupted by Leslie's departure, displaying a remarkable knowledge of the Dead Sea Scrolls.

I am no longer interested in the Dead Sea Scrolls. With a skillful maneuver I manage to shift our conversation to his person and discover that the intriguing stranger is from Morocco, North Africa.

"Morocco?" I am beguiled. "I have never met anyone from Morocco or North Africa. Which city?"

"Casablanca."

"Oh, Casablanca, the city of intrigue, of romance and of the Casbah!" I mimic a deep sigh, and put my hand over my heart.

"How do you know?" He seems genuinely surprised.

"From the movie *Casablanca* with Ingrid Bergman and Humphrey Bogart!"

"Ah yes."

The train is pulling into Kings Highway Station, and I rise.

"This is where I get off." I extend my hand. "*Shalom.* It was nice meeting you."

A bright smile lights up the oval face as he springs to his feet.

"What a coincidence! Kings Highway is also my stop! We are getting off together," he says in biblical Hebrew. "May I?"

He extends his hand to take my briefcase and, carrying it like a trophy, follows me out of the subway car, down the stairs, and out of the station into a brisk October wind.

I must rush, and reach for my briefcase with a sense of urgency.

"Thank you. It was truly nice meeting you."

The tall Moroccan seems reluctant to part with my briefcase, and when I snatch it from his hand he seems somewhat abashed. "Are you in a hurry?"

"Yes, very."

"May I walk with you? We can continue our talk on the way to your house."

"I'm sorry, but I must run. It's Friday afternoon. . . . It's quite late. I must help my mother with preparations for the Sabbath. You see, I am religiously observant. . . ."

"How extraordinary!" he exclaims. "So am I. Another coincidence! But I must confess I would have never thought that you were. You don't look . . . I would've never thought you were Jewish even. You're so white—I mean blond."

I wave my briefcase in the air, laughing. "I really must run."

"Wait! I don't even know your name."

He reaches into an inside pocket for a pen, and is

ready to write on the margin of a rolled-up newspaper under his arm.

"May I have your phone number?"

The pen is out of ink, and no matter how hard he presses down he manages to produce nothing but a number of illegible scrapings.

"Shabbat Shalom!" I shout, and waving farewell with my briefcase, take off at a run. Suddenly I remember: I forgot to ask his name! As I stop in my tracks and turn back, I can see him still fumbling with his useless pen, his newspaper now propped against the wall of Dubrow's Café.

"What's your name?" I shout into the raging wind.

The head with the crown of dark waves turns, bits of sound travel in the wind, shreds of sound, unintelligible fragments reach me. I cannot make them out, but I cannot tarry. I must run. It's near sundown.

What is the name of this tall, dark, captivating stranger? I may never know.

Will he succeed in deciphering my name and telephone number on the margin of his newspaper? Will he try?

If he doesn't, I may never see him again.

Chapter Twenty-Seven

MY AMERICAN HIGH SCHOOL DIPLOMA

"It's for you." Mother hands me the telephone receiver, and her face is an open question mark. "Some fellow . . . David something."

"Hello? Who is this?"

"Miss Friedman? I hope you remember me. We met on the subway train . . . on Friday afternoon. Remember?"

It is the tall, dark stranger! So he did manage to decipher my name and my phone number on the margin of his newspaper . . . wasted no time to make contact . . . I'm impressed.

"Hello? I am sorry if I am disturbing you, but are you the young lady I met on the subway? Do I have the right number?"

"Oh yes, you do. This is the right number. I'm the girl you met on the Brighton Line. But I didn't catch your name."

"My name is David Bitton."

"Pleased to meet you. Please call me Leah. That's my Hebrew name."

"Thank you. Leah . . . I wish to remind you: We have not finished our discussion. Can we meet and continue where we left off? Are you free tonight?"

"Tonight?" I remember Sally's warning: Never agree to a date on the same day as asked. I also remember that Alex phoned from Rochester saying he would be back home today and might drop in for a visit. I have not seen him for several weeks. He has been working on a research project in hematology at the Mayo Clinic in Rochester, New York. On the phone he sounded happy and excited, eager to tell me all about it.

"I'm sorry, I'm not free tonight. But let me see. . . ."

"How about tomorrow evening?"

Tomorrow evening I have a class at Erasmus Hall. "I'm truly sorry, I'm not free tomorrow evening either. . . ."

"What about Tuesday, then?"

"I have an idea. I have two tickets for the Adlai Stevenson rally at the Madison Square Garden on Tuesday evening. Do you want to come? Are you interested in the presidential campaign?"

"I don't know much about it. But I would love to come to the rally."

I got the tickets from my brother, who has been working as a campaign volunteer. It could be fun to attend a rally for a presidential candidate.

David Bitton and I have designated as our meeting place a corner on Fifth Avenue near Rockefeller Center. When I emerge from the subway station I am stunned by the swarming multitude on the avenue. How will I find him in this throng? How will I spot his face in this sea of faces? How will I recognize him?

I rise on tiptoes and crane my neck to scan the surface of the human deep. All at once above the crowd I catch sight of a gray fedora and an arm waving a folded newspaper in the air. Can it be him? The features below the hat do not resemble those of the dark stranger I met in the subway. Yet the tall man in the gray fedora keeps waving the folded newspaper, and now is making his way in my direction. Ah, I can see the paper in his hand is the Hebrew weekly *HaDoar*. As he approaches he raises his hat and flashes a smile, and I recognize the crown of dark wavy hair, the somewhat shy yet provocative smile.

"Hello, David!" I shout. "I'm glad you've made it."

"And I'm glad we found each other," he shouts back. "Do you know which way to Madison Square Garden?"

"This way. Follow me." Mustering every ounce of determination, I begin to forge a path in the crowd, and David makes a valiant effort to follow. But we seem to make no progress battling the crowd. Our endeavors in the face of overwhelming throngs of Stevenson followers seem hopeless. Ultimately our exertions to reach the building where the rally is taking place are doomed to failure, my prize tickets are not utilized, and I do not meet my brother's idol in person as I had hoped. We cannot even hear his speech broadcast over the loudspeakers: It is drowned out by the incessant ovation of the crowd.

All evening long David and I are swept back and forth by the burgeoning multitude. Drifting with jubilant Stevenson fans on the streets of midtown

Manhattan becomes the history of our first date.

But all is not lost. The homebound Brighton train eventually becomes an enclave for a quiet reunion. In the privacy of our subway niche we continue our encounter begun last Friday, slowly, cautiously prying personal tidbits from each other, about each other. With mounting excitement we get to know each other, and embark on the tentative birth of a relationship.

I am fascinated to learn that David Bitton's mother tongue is Arabic and his second language is French. That his parents live in Marrakech, Morocco's royal city, his two younger sisters in the capital Rabbat, while a half-brother in Meknez in the Atlas Mountains. I learn that he himself came from Morocco three years ago, and is a student and a teacher just like me.

By the time the train pulls into our station on Kings Highway, it is too late to go anywhere but home. This time David Bitton walks me to Ocean Avenue, and takes his leave at the entrance of our building. I do not invite him in: It is not done on the first date.

We have been dating for a month now, and David has asked me to be his steady date. Say *yes,* say *yes,* say *yes*— becomes the tenor of our every rendezvous.

Every day I find an envelope in our mailbox, and the envelope contains a Hebrew poem, a different poem each day, a different declaration of love, a passionate plea to make him the happiest man on earth and say yes. . . . A prayer to end his agony and become his steady date— to become only *his!*

As I open each envelope my hands tremble a little and my heart skips a beat with anticipation.

Should I say yes? Is David Bitton, in the words of Sally and Evelyn, Mr. Right?

The "Friedman gang" likes him but is concerned about his "mysterious" background.

"Try to find out more about his family, about the place he comes from," Mother cautions.

"His background is so different from ours," Uncle Martin complains. "Why can't you date someone who belongs to our milieu?"

"He's very handsome and very charming," Aunt Celia warns, as if handsome and charming were a disease.

"Get to know him better," my brother advises. "Take your time, *Leanyka*. Don't be impetuous. It takes time to get to know a guy."

The barrage of poems has a cumulative effect, and I believe . . . I believe I'm going to say yes soon. Oh, God, help me, what should I do?

Bubi barges into the house and disrupts my quiet deliberations.

"You know what? My new roommate was admitted to Yeshiva University with a High School Equivalency Diploma," he announces. "This diploma, issued by the University of the State of New York, qualifies students for college entrance who for some reason had not finished high school."

"But this is precisely my case!" I cry with great agitation. "Don't you think?"

"Of course. That's the reason I'm telling you about it,"

Bubi says with a knowing smile. "That's the reason I found out all about it."

"What did you find out?"

"That there are preparatory courses for the exam, free of charge, and both the courses and the exams are administered at Washington Irving High School in Lower Manhattan. You too can take these courses, and then take the exam for the diploma. If you pass, and I am sure you will, you can enter college."

"Oh, Bubi, that's great! You're simply wonderful! Thanks. But how do I go about it?"

"Why don't you call Washington Irving High School tomorrow during your lunch hour and find out when the courses begin? Then take it from there."

Instead of telephoning I cut my lunch short and take the subway downtown to Washington Irving High School to inquire in person. The preoccupied secretary at the front desk is much too busy to answer my questions about course schedules; she focuses her attention on directing applicants to the auditorium for the High School Equivalency Examination that is to start in ten minutes.

What? The examination I have come to inquire about is to start just now? What should I do?

"When is the next exam?" I ask the harried secretary.

"Some time next year."

"Can anyone take the exam today?" I ask again, my voice turning thin with anxiety.

"Anyone who has five dollars for the examination fee can take the test," comes the startling reply.

Five dollars? Frantically rummaging in my purse, I find enough change to make up the five dollars!

"Here, miss, five dollars in change. Is that acceptable? I want to take the exam now."

"You have to pay the fee at the bursar's counter. Come back with the receipt and I'll put you on the list."

I am the only customer at the bursar's counter. I pay the fee, and within minutes my name is entered on the list of applicants. Then, without allowing myself to think twice, I walk directly into the examination hall, buzzing with nervous tension.

The examination is to take five hours, the monitor announces, during which time there is no talking, no smoking, no eating. We can leave the room only with permission. Suddenly reality strikes. What am I doing? Am I in my right mind to undertake a series of tests without preparation, without an idea of what to expect?

I look around me. The students in my proximity talk to each other. They know each other; they have just completed a preparatory course for these examinations together. But me, I am to face an array of subjects I know nothing about.

Instruction sheets are distributed, and then question sheets, pages and pages of questions. There are many words that are foreign to me, questions I don't understand. For the next five hours I wage a battle of concentration, reading and rereading questions, focusing on memory, on things learned long ago, formulating answers in English, carefully crafting English sentences.

When the exam is over I am drained of my last ounce

of energy. And I am faint with hunger.

"Tomorrow morning all of you be here at nine sharp," the exam monitor announces.

"What?" To my horror I discover that today's examination was only the first part. The second part—math, geometry, history, and economics—is scheduled for 9:00 to 12:00 tomorrow. How can I take a day off without explanation? And there is no time to explain, to phone for permission. What am I to do?

Bubi once again comes to my rescue. He agrees to telephone the principal at the yeshiva tomorrow morning and explain everything, offering to substitute for me in class. I have great confidence in Bubi's intercession, and go off to take the second part of the examination with a lighter heart.

Two weeks later, in the mailbox under the familiar pale blue folder containing David's latest love poem, I find a manila envelope. In it is my high school diploma, straight from Albany, the capital of New York State. What a beautiful document! Above the bright gold seal of the University of the State of New York Education Department and the signature of the Acting Associate Commissioner of Education Frederick G. Moffito, in fancy calligraphy it states that *having satisfactorily completed the comprehensive examination requirements prescribed by the Commissioner of Education, Elvira L. Friedman is thereby entitled to this High School Equivalency Diploma.*

Isn't it simply wonderful? I can barely believe it. I have a high school diploma, the first bona fide qualification for my higher education. My passport to college! My first academic achievement in America!

I must share my ecstatic joy with someone or I'll burst!

Mommy, Aunt Celia, and Uncle Martin are at work. Bubi has classes at this hour, and I can't reach him either. Whom can I tell? Sally and Evelyn? But they too are at work for at least another hour. Should I call Alex? Or perhaps David Bitton? But neither Alex nor David approves of my fervent ambition to study. They would not understand what this diploma truly means to me.

Snatching my bright red coolie coat from the closet I run down the stairs, out into the street. Ocean Avenue is basking in the golden rays of the late afternoon sun, and I feel like embracing its radiance, clutching it to my bosom together with my diploma. At a run I head for the little park on the corner of Kings Highway and Bedford Avenue, and there, under a cluster of maple trees, I slump onto a bench.

"I've done it! I've done it!" I shout to the trees, to the brisk breeze, to the gossamer clouds sailing across a pale blue sky.

I've done it, Papa! The first stage of a fervent dream has come true! Papa, I know it is also your dream. I know you want me to get a higher education. I want to do it for you, Papa!

A steady stream of cars and trucks are rolling past me on Kings Highway, but all I hear is the sound of departing horses' hooves and the fading clatter of carriage wheels. All I see is the silhouette of your tall, slim torso vanishing into the distance.

Papa, for me you're not gone. You're near me, within me forever.

Tears are trickling down my cheeks from under closed eyelids.

I want you to be proud of me, Papa!